Medical Library Association

MLA

Focus Groups for Libraries and Librarians

Beryl Glitz

Forbes

CUSTOM PUBLISHING

60 FIFTH AVE · NEW YORK, NY · 10011

CIP Data is available.
Printed in the United States of America
10 9 8 7 6 5 4 3 2 1

ISBN 0–8281–1249–5

INTRODUCTION

⚜

For many of us, our experience with focus groups starts with a telephone call from a marketing company conducting a survey. They might ask us where we do our banking, what kind of car we drive, or if we ever go on holiday abroad. If we are lucky enough to answer "correctly," according to the criteria demanded by the sponsor, we are asked to attend a "focus group" at a local office and might be offered $40, $50, or even $150 for a few hours of our time. If we accept the offer we would, for an evening, be part of a large and prospering industry that taps into consumer views of products and services. Companies with businesses ranging from manufacturing automatic coffee makers to offering tropical island vacations all use the technique to find out what will sell and how it might best be sold, simply by listening to the people who would be doing the buying.

While this is perhaps the best known face of the focus group technique, it has long been used by social sciences researchers for gathering qualitative data in order to understand people's ideas, feelings, perceptions, and beliefs. The technique involves a small group of individuals, brought together by a moderator to discuss a topic of which they all have some knowledge, interest, or experience. Through a series of open ended questions, the moderator leads the discussion, encouraging both free expression of ideas and interaction among the participants. In this way, the moderator can learn how group members honestly feel about the topic.

As a research method, the focus group's success lies in its ability to draw out what is on people's minds, rather than forcing them to respond to what is on the researcher's mind. Because of this, it can be a useful method for conducting evaluative research. It is perhaps not surprising, then, that focus groups should have proved so popular in the competitive worlds of marketing and advertising, as a way to understand how consumers view their products. And in the last twenty years, because of economic constraints and increasing pressure to justify the resources they use, service organizations have also turned to focus groups to measure the effectiveness and efficiency of their own products, namely, the services they provide, as well as to better understand the needs of their clients.

Libraries, like any other service organization, want to provide their users with the types of services that best meet their needs. The focus group has significant potential in the library environment as a method for gathering qualitative data to assess those needs and understand how well the library is fulfilling them. By revealing how users, and non-users, view their services, the focus group interview can help library staff learn what is needed to improve existing services, gain insight and guidance for developing new services, and thus make any necessary changes in the most cost effective way. This makes the focus group technique an important tool in strategic planning. Moreover, apart from its practical use in measuring library performance and making management decisions, the focus group has some side benefits that should be considered. Involving users in these groups can help develop a very positive image of the library among users and strengthen their perceptions of themselves as important stakeholders in the library's ongoing existence and future development. Users will be more inclined to support and, if necessary, fight for an institution that listens to them and involves them in decision making than one that does not appear sensitive to their needs. Participation of librarians in focus groups with library users can also make the staff individually and collectively much more aware and appreciative of how the library is viewed by its clients.

This book is intended as a basic introduction and guide to using focus group interviewing in the library. It provides the rationale for employing such a methodology, using in-house staff, where normally there is little money or time available for qualitative data collection. It will also serve as a practical manual for those who wish to conduct focus groups with library clientele. The book draws on the author's own experience in organizing focus groups; the experience of colleagues, particularly those within the Regional Medical Library; discussions with other librarians who have used the technique; a quantitative survey of medical libraries with respect to their use of focus groups; and a comprehensive consideration of the extensive literature on the use of the technique in libraries and in the broader context of advertising, commerce, and social science research.

The first five chapters provide background information on the use of the technique followed by chapters that explain the steps included in conducting a focus group project: selecting a moderator, preparing the questions, selecting the participants, moderating and recording the discussion, analyzing and reporting the results, and using the findings. The book concludes with a final chapter that describes two case studies of focus group projects in the library setting, along with examples of actual questions used. The information in this book should help library managers understand the proper use of the technique and apply it successfully to a whole range of library issues and concerns.

Acknowledgments

I want to express my thanks and appreciation to the many librarians in health sciences libraries who have helped contribute to this book by sharing their experiences and insight into the use of focus groups, through responses to my survey and discussions about their focus group projects. Special thanks must go to Claire Hamasu and Alison Bunting, my colleagues in the Pacific Southwest Regional Medical Library, and to Clara Chu, from the UCLA Graduate School of Education and Information Science, who provided both encouragement and practical suggestions for this work. I also appreciated the help of Jane Thomsen of Carson-Tahoe Hospital who provided useful commentary from the hospital library perspective. Most of all I want to thank my husband, Dohn Glitz, who endured the many ups and downs of a first-time book author. His active encouragement, thoughtful readings of manuscript drafts, and practical editorial advice were of enormous benefit and support.

CONTENTS

1

FOCUS GROUP INTERVIEWING: A QUALITATIVE RESEARCH METHOD

The focus group interview is a technique originally developed by social scientists to gather data on the opinions, knowledge, perceptions and concerns of small groups of individuals about a particular topic. The major contribution of the technique lies in the fact that small-group process encourages people to express their views in a way that other methods cannot [1]. The interaction among the group members often leads to revelations and opinions that may not have been brought out in individual interviews and would not have had the opportunity to be considered in more controlled approaches such as through the use of written questionnaires. All sorts of uses can be made of this type of discussion: from designing the best type of packaging for toothpaste to developing techniques to encourage family planning; from under-standing voter attitudes to political candidates to designing an online public catalog for a university library. By carefully analyzing the data resulting from the discussion, the researcher can gain insight into how the topic is perceived by the group, whether it concerns a product, a service, an attitude, or a formal research project.

The term "focus group" is sometimes loosely used to describe various small group interactions that involve decision making, consensus building, or conflict resolution within the group. This type of interaction, however, is not truly a focus group discussion since its goal is normally reached *at the conclusion* of the discussion. As it is used here, the term "focus group" is defined as a method for generating data or information, within the small group setting, which, *when analyzed*, can help in: planning; making decisions; evaluating programs, products, or services; developing models or theories; enriching the findings from other research methods; and constructing questionnaires for further data gathering. This book will concentrate on the focus group as a mechanism through which library management can gain a better understanding of the needs and expectations of their patrons and their own success or failure in meeting those needs.

Focus Group Structure: A focus group typically consists of between six and ten individuals who have some knowledge of or experience with the topic under discussion, or who share certain characteristics that are related to that topic. For example, in the library these individuals might be students who need space for study and research, or medical staff who are interested in access to online journal information. The relatively homogeneous group is led by a skilled and knowledgeable moderator whose job is to introduce the topic and facilitate discussion. The moderator guides the participants through a series of questions. These questions have been carefully prepared and are posed in a somewhat structured yet open-ended format designed to bring out the honest opinions of the group. An equally important role for the moderator is to ensure that all members of the group participate, and to encourage discussion among them. In this way, a wide variety of viewpoints are expressed on the topic.

TABLE 1–1

FOCUS GROUP CHARACTERISTICS
- Small group—6–10 people
- Members share knowledge, experience, or characteristics
- Moderator leads discussion
- Group interaction is encouraged
- Questions are open-ended

As a method for gathering data, the focus group approach is grounded in two basic assumptions: because individuals are able to verbalize their thoughts and feelings, they can be important sources of information; the dynamics of a group not only bring out more and better information than individual interviews, but also ensure the validity of the information contributed [2]. By drawing out, analyzing and responding to specific comments, the group reinforces or negates individual opinions. The frank and open discussion that develops from these interactions among group members can provide an accurate picture of their underlying attitudes and behavioral approach. As such, focus groups provide important clues as to "how" and "why" people think and act the way they do [3].

Because of the nature of a focus group, however, information gathered by this method cannot be described as truly representative of the population at large. It is, quite simply, the expressed opinions of a group of individuals. Nor can it be said to reflect the strength of the feelings or opinions expressed [4]. To make any kind of projections from the results, many groups would need to be convened because individual groups consist of too small a number of people. Nor are members necessarily selected on a strictly scientific basis. They are chosen simply because they share some common characteristics that are significantly related to the topic of the discussion and they are willing to expend the time and effort to make their opinions known. Rather, the importance of the focus group is in the unique type of information gathered. Since the technique encourages free expression of group members' honest opinions and experiences yet keeps the discussion focused on the topic, the information gathered can provide a good reflection of how people really feel about a subject. In essence, the results of a focus group discussion allow those using the technique to experience reality in the same manner as the participants. Given this ability, the focus group technique has proved to be an effective method for gathering qualitative data in a variety of research settings.

Qualitative Research: Focus group interviewing is only one of a number of qualitative methods used to gather empirical data in research projects. The qualitative approach, in general, involves listening, questioning, and observing as ways of collecting data [5]. Other methods include in-depth or one-on-one interviews, written documents such as diaries, narratives, or life histories, and participant observation. They are all concerned with recording feelings, experiences, and impressions and it is the subjects' own words, either spoken or written, which make up the data to be studied. These data are then carefully analyzed so that the researcher can develop new hypotheses or modify existing knowledge. Because of their focus on personal experience rather than the use of proscribed response categories, qualitative methods such as the focus group can provide the human dimension to research that quantitative methods often lack.

In contrast, the quantitative approach to data gathering relies on numbers to describe concepts and opinions. The written questionnaire is an example of a quantitative method that is widely used in both formal and informal research projects. It provides a systematic and standardized way of gathering data, through the use of predetermined categories into which all responses must fit. These data are then used to either prove or disprove an existing hypothesis. Typically, quantitative methods draw on a large number of respondents, often carefully selected to be representative of a larger group. And, because of their mathematical formulation, the results of quantitative research can easily be compared, aggregated statistically, and projected to represent the population at large.

In formal research projects, qualitative techniques are often used in conjunction with quantitative ones. This is referred to as triangulation and can involve not only the use of different methods, but also different researchers or data sources, in the study of a particular subject. In his description of the theoretical framework on which the focus group is based, Calder demonstrated this interaction of different methodologies. He identified three major approaches to the focus group methodology: exploratory, clinical, and phenomenological [6]. The first, exploratory, is primarily used in pilot testing or for generating hypotheses or theories, which are then tested with other methodologies. In this approach, the focus group studies would typically be followed by some type of quantitative technique, such as a questionnaire, to test the hypotheses developed. In the library, a focus group might indicate that its participants, for example, felt the need for formal training sessions to properly utilize CD-ROM products. Questionnaire results could then verify and quantitate this need, detailing perhaps the types of users likely to attend, and the most popular times for classes.

The clinical approach to focus groups, on the other hand, is used to study the underlying, psychological motivations for people's behaviors and attitudes. As such, this method of discussion would generally be used after some other type of study has been conducted, in order to explore more fully certain findings. To reverse our example above, data from a questionnaire could demonstrate a widespread interest among library users in receiving training for CD-ROM products. A focus group could then probe why the users felt this was necessary, what they felt they could learn, and, in general, discover user reactions to this medium. The third approach, labeled phenomenological by Calder, is used to explore the opinions and experiences of group members, so that the moderator is able to see the world from their point of view. It provides a direct link between the providers and the users of a product or service. Typically, this type of discussion would be more focused and generate more specific responses, and would be repeated with several different groups until no new information is forthcoming. In our example it could be used to evaluate the success of the training sessions, exploring the subsequent level of use of the product by attendees, their comfort level with the product, and their potential interest in further training.

Although the three approaches delineated by Calder can be distinguished from one another by their purpose, in practice there is much overlap. For the library, any of these approaches can be potentially helpful. Focus groups can generate useful information, either used alone or in conjunction with other methods [7]. Using them before conducting a formal survey will help develop potential questions that might otherwise have been overlooked. Held after a survey has been conducted, they provide the means of further investigating specific results or questions that have emerged from analysis of the quantitative data gathered. Used alone, they can provide useful information on how the library's services and administration are viewed by patrons or staff.

A Library Application: The following hypothetical situation may help explain the differences between qualitative and quantitative approaches to gathering data and provide an example of how focus groups might be used in the library setting. A university library in which a CD-ROM network has recently been installed to increase access to online databases may wish to determine how well its patrons are able to use this new service. Library staff may decide to employ a user survey to determine their level of satisfaction with the CD-ROM system, and to discover what types of search problems individuals are experiencing. With a well-designed questionnaire the library could learn a great deal about these users, including university status, age, prior searching experience, etc. The survey could also help to determine the degree of satisfaction of each group. Results might show, for instance, that while overall satisfaction was high, students were much more satisfied with the new system than faculty members. Data might also reveal that subject searching was viewed as more difficult than author or title searching.

While such data could help library staff to pinpoint problem areas and determine which group of users might need special attention in effectively utilizing the CD-ROM network, it could not provide any real insight, for example, into just why the faculty had such a negative response. Additional questions might help identify problems which faculty typically encounter in searching, *e.g.*, difficulty in using certain features or strong competition for workstations. The reasons given, however, would be limited to the response categories delineated on the questionnaire. A space for open-ended comments might provide some spontaneous answers, but busy users may not take the time to add them. Respondents, in fact, would be primarily using the library's reasons, not their own, to register dissatisfaction. The comparison is similar to the relationship between a multiple-choice and a written or oral examination. In the multiple-choice format, a number of possible answers are provided by the teacher and one or more must be selected. In the essay or oral format, the student must formulate a response with little or no guidance or limitation. In the example given, by using a qualitative approach, such as a focus group, library staff could learn from the faculty, in their own words, the nature of their problems in searching the CD-ROM system. Such a group might in fact reveal that while there are frequent classes, free and open to everyone, provided to help people in using the new system, faculty feel uncomfortable in attending these classes. Extended discussion might prove that it is precisely because the groups are open to anyone that faculty do not attend; they are concerned that they might have to reveal their lack of knowledge and their discomfort with computers to their own students.

Information such as this could not easily be elicited from a survey questionnaire. Only in a group of peers might faculty be expected to offer this sort of self-revelation. Yet it is precisely the kind of information that could help library staff take appropriate action. Rather than developing more elaborate teaching methods or scheduling class sessions at different times, the library could tailor its response to meet genuine need. By providing individual training sessions or faculty-only classes, for example, library staff would more effectively address the concerns of this particular group of users.

As illustrated by this hypothetical example, the focus group technique can clearly benefit libraries and other service organizations by providing a relatively simple research method for better understanding the users' needs. Such an understanding can lead to better management decisions to help satisfy those needs.

Credibility of the Data: In any type of research project, a major concern is for the quality of the data collected. In the library setting, this is especially true when the data will be used to make important decisions that can result in significant changes or expenditures. In quantitative research approaches, two major criteria regularly used for testing the accuracy of the data are reliability and validity. The former refers to the ability of the tool used to measure accurately and consistently what is being studied, while the latter is concerned with how closely the data reflect the purpose of the research and represent reality. While some researchers feel that these are not appropriate terms to use in evaluating qualitative methods, clearly some criteria are needed to judge the believability of the data collected and the methods used. Holloway and

Wheeler in their discussion of appropriate terminology for validating qualitative methods, suggest other measures [8]. They describe the importance of establishing 'trustworthiness' of the data through the tests of credibility, transferability, dependability, and confirmability. They believe these four criteria can be established when: a knowledgeable individual is conducting the research; appropriate participants are selected; sufficient time is spent with those providing the data; results are checked for accuracy with participants and with peers; procedures are clearly defined; and the conclusions drawn are shown to be taken directly from the data and could therefore presumably be reached by an independent researcher. They stress the importance of what has been referred to as an "audit trail," which provides an accurate record of the data, how they were collected, and how conclusions were drawn from that evidence. Thus a reliable focus group discussion is much more than a "bull session"; it is open ended yet carefully organized, directed toward a specific problem, comprehensive in its content, and ultimately will clearly document and justify any conclusions that may be reached.

TABLE 1–2

QUALITATIVE DATA CREDIBILITY CHECKS

- Project goals are clear and understandable
- Procedures are planned and documented
- Appropriate participants are selected
- Moderator is competent and knowledgeable
- Questions are unambiguous and open-ended
- Data are accurately recorded
- All pertinent data are used for the analysis

Given the nature of qualitative research, the Holloway and Wheeler criteria seem highly appropriate. Whatever the terminology used, the major goal is to protect the integrity of the data through each step of the research project [9]. In the focus group setting, this involves the skills of the moderator, the quality of the questions asked, the suitability of the participants, and the accuracy of the data analysis. All of these have a significant effect on the outcome of the project. Because of their importance, much of the remainder of this book will be devoted to a detailed consideration of these aspects of focus group interviewing. Later chapters will show how the value of the data gathered can be improved by the skills and sensitivity of the interviewer, the selection of group members, a systematic and thoughtful approach to constructing and asking questions, and a thorough and careful content analysis. Attention to these factors supports the development of useful and believable results. The same care is needed in developing and using quantitative methods such as questionnaires. Although the reliability and validity of the data cannot be judged in the same way that quantitative findings are, qualitative data can be credible if kept in proper context. Hence the focus group method can be successfully used as a formal research tool by social scientists studying human values and behavior, and as a more informal method for use by program and service organizations, including libraries, in planning and evaluation.

REFERENCES

1. Kitzinger J. Introducing focus groups. BMJ 1995 July 29; 311(7000):299–302.
2. Lederman LC. Assessing educational effectiveness: the focus group interview as a technique for data collection. Commun Ed 1990 Apr; 39(2):117–27.
3. Folch-Lyon E, Trost JF. Conducting focus group sessions. Studies in Family Planning 1981 Dec; 12(12):443–9.
4. Basch CE. Focus group interview: an underutilized research technique for improving theory and practice in health education. Health Ed Q 1987 Win;14(4):414.
5. Holloway I, Wheeler, S. Qualitative research for nurses. Oxford: Blackwell Scientific, 1996.
6. Calder BJ. Focus groups and the nature of qualitative marketing research. J Marketing Res 1977;14:353–64.
7. Glitz B. The focus group technique in library research: an introduction. Bull Med Libr Assoc 1997 Oct; 85(4):385–90.
8. Holloway, Wheeler, op. cit.
9. Mays N, Pope C. Rigour and qualitative research. BMJ 1995 July 29; 311(7000):109–12.

2

How Focus Groups Work:
The Small Group Process

As a qualitative research method, the focus group interview depends for its effectiveness on successful group formation and interaction. While the moderator who leads the group can and does affect these to some degree, it is the interaction between the actual participants that makes this methodology both valuable and unique. While much has been written on the phenomenon of group dynamics, it would be useful here to briefly review the nature of groups and how they are formed. An understanding of this process can assist those using the focus group technique to take advantage of the various steps in group development to both enhance that development and encourage full participation by its members. It is also important to understand the role of the moderator in this process and how that individual can influence both the formation of the group and its ultimate success.

Group Definition: In his study of the psychology of small groups, Shaw draws together the various definitions of a group that are frequently based on specific group characteristics, including motivation, group goals, or how the group is organized. Striving for a more general approach, Shaw himself defines the group as "two or more persons who are interacting with one another in such a manner that each person influences and is influenced by each other person" [1]. Kurt Lewin first labeled this influence and interaction as "group dynamics" in the 1930s. Because of this interchange between group members, the group will develop a "personality" of its own and thus it will potentially produce a wider insight and broader perspective than individuals could achieve on their own. This phenomenon of group dynamics can produce useful information in a setting such as the focus group. In fact it is the underlying basis and rationale for using the technique. The opinion given by one group member brings a reaction from another member, which can lead to further insight and broader understanding of the topic. Individuals respond to one another, perhaps modify their own opinions, and yet they are free not to reach a common agreement or understanding. These are the features that make a focus group discussion work and differentiate the technique from the other major qualitative methodology, the individual interview.

The fact that focus groups are also small groups is a second underlying factor that contributes to their success. While there appears to be no exact number for membership included in small group definitions, Hare sees the defining characteristic as the opportunity for face-to-face interaction between each member [2]. The typical number of focus group participants, six to ten individuals, is sufficient to give a range of ideas and opinions and to allow real participation and discussion by all, while preventing domination or intimidation by any one member of the group. This small group interaction, which lies at the heart of the focus group's success, depends upon the successful transformation of the various individuals into a collective whole. Such a transformation generally takes place in a series of steps which together constitute group process.

Group Process: Group process is defined by Gordon and Langmaid as that sequence of developmental stages through which the group passes simply as a result of being a group and wanting to communicate with one another [3]. Although the exact nature of this development will vary from group to group depending on its goals, function, etc., Tuckman identified a typical sequence of four unique phases in group development, which he labeled *forming, storming, norming, and performing* [4]. Gordon and Langmaid also identified a fifth phase, *mourning*.

Forming, the initial stage of the process, begins when members first start to think of themselves as part of the group and gain some understanding of each other and the task ahead of them. In a typical focus group it will occupy the first fifteen to twenty minutes of the session. This is an extremely important part of the process because it is critical that every member is made to feel included and will therefore want to contribute. It is also one in which the moderator can have an active influence. For example, if some members of the group already know one another and have an established relationship—*e.g.*, supervisor and employee, newcomer and long-time employee, teacher and student—the moderator may need to establish that all of their opinions and ideas are equally interesting and important.

Perhaps the easiest way to accomplish forming is to have each member of the group say something, preferably in the first five to ten minutes. In the focus group, an easy way to do this is through self-introductions, going quickly around the room and giving each person a chance to speak. This activity serves to "break the ice" and relieve individual anxiety. Moreover, by making everyone speak out, it prevents anyone from feeling excluded. Another method is to start with a very simple question and, rather than waiting for volunteers, ask each person in turn to answer. Again, this forces participation, makes it clear to all members of the group that each of them is expected to contribute, and demonstrates that all opinions and ideas will be heard.

Although it takes time, forming is vitally important because it encourages participants to feel and behave as a part of the group and to see it as a place where they can speak out and be listened to. Since this is the whole point of a focus group discussion, forming is probably the most critical stage. If some individuals do not participate in the process, they can quickly feel rejected. Consequently the rest of the group may react to them and this reaction can easily affect the discussion process. On the one hand, the larger group might try to disassociate themselves from the rejected members, either by deliberate disagreement with their opinions or by ignoring their input. On the other hand, the larger group might develop a group defense to "rescue" the isolated members, which could also skew the discussion by too much agreement or even by setting up antagonism between the moderator and the group. Either way, the openness and frankness of the discussion may be diminished.

The second stage, *storming*, refers to the inevitable working out of power and control that occurs amongst the group members. This is the process through which individuals learn about each other and how the group is going to function: who knows how much; who is assertive; who is passive; who has the most status; etc. This is the stage at which the moderator will begin to develop some appreciation for the person-alities of the group members and some strategies for assuring their participation in the group process. It is also the time when group members learn about the moderator, how active or passive his or her participation will be and just what role this individual will play. Storming is extremely important since it helps the group members decide how they can best interrelate with one another and with the moderator. It is the time for setting boundaries and establishing the norms, the rules of behavior, by which the group will operate in the allotted time. Moderators should not be alarmed at the interactions between group members during this stage, nor should they attempt to directly intervene. The group needs to establish its own identity and mores, and to feel that members are expected to listen and react to one another—that they are in fact a group and not simply a collection of individuals. However, the moderator needs to be aware of what is happening during this process and should use the opportunity to identify individuals who could create problems for the group either by attempting to dominate the conversation or by withdrawing from the group interaction. Hopefully, storming will be limited to just a few moments of the session. While it may be a time of some tension as members jockey for position, storming is an essential part of the process if the group is to go on to the next stage and get down to the proper business at hand.

This third stage, *norming*, is characterized by an easing of tension and a general acceptance of each other by the group members. Individuals will have learned that they have at least some things in common and will have a general idea of how members are likely to react. They will have also learned that the moderator is interested in hearing a variety of opinions, and not in seeking consensus or a "correct" response. People will relax, perhaps shift closer to one another, and in general their body language will show that they now see themselves as a group [5]. It is at this point when members are most willing to talk to one another. A good moderator will recognize when this stage has been reached and will be ready to quickly lead the group into its most productive stage, *performing*.

In the focus group, this fourth stage of group development is where the real discussion takes place and, if the group has truly coalesced, the moderator will be able to step back and let the members take more responsibility for keeping the discussion going. However, if and when a different topic is introduced by the moderator, the group may well revert to an earlier stage, and further storming may occur until new norms have been determined by the group. When this happens, if the moderator understands the process, he or she will not feel that the group is starting to break down and try to intervene. Instead, the moderator can trust the group to work through this stage as they did in the previous topic discussion. However, the moderator may be able to accelerate this process and more quickly return the group to the performing mode.

The final stage in the group process, *mourning*, comes when the group begins to acknowledge that time and energy are running out and the group must disband. It is important for the moderator to take the lead in this acknowledgment and provide participants with the opportunity of winding down their discussion. Gordon and Langmaid advocate leaving the last few minutes for members to recap their group experiences, either by offering some final words, modifying any earlier remarks, or adding something they had perhaps wanted to say. This process allows the group to come to closure and its members to leave with a feeling of satisfaction that they have accomplished their discussion goals. Such personal satisfaction is important in two ways: future recruitment for focus groups will be easier if participants believe their efforts have been worthwhile, and the institution sponsoring the discussion can benefit from members' feelings of inclusion and importance that effective participation can engender.

Groups that exist over an extended period of time and meet on numerous occasions, such as a committee or club, will have greater opportunity to work through these different stages. Focus groups, however, which only come together for one or two hours, must progress more rapidly if they are to at least reach the performing stage and carry on a productive discussion. While most groups develop in the manner described, members are usually not conscious that they are exhibiting the different behaviors of each stage, nor do they necessarily know under which stage their group is operating at any given time. The moderator, however, should be very much aware of them and of the group's transition through each one, in order to use them to advantage. While each stage reflects different needs of the group, all of them have an impact on the discussion.

Group Structure and Content: While some of what occurs during these five stages of group process is to a significant degree out of the hands of the moderator, two other major components of group discussion are more directly controllable: structure and content [6]. The first, structure, refers to the various physical factors associated with a group. These include the time, place, and length of the discussion; the number and qualifications of the participants; the similarities and differences of experience and behavior of the participants; the type and arrangement of the seating; the ambiance of the setting; and the choice of moderator. Because these are the "tangibles" of a group discussion, the things which members see and experience, they can have an important impact on the group's functioning. Fortunately these factors can often be closely controlled by the individual conducting the focus group project. Later chapters will discuss issues concerning many of these structural components since they can seriously affect the successful outcome of the focus group.

A second component, content, refers to the subject matter, the order in which topics are discussed, and techniques used in the discussion itself. Because content is also very much under the control of those conducting the focus group project, further chapters will explore in more detail the importance of good content preparation in order to get the best results from the discussion. Whatever approach is used: a general discussion, based on a topic outline; a set of specific questions; the use of special techniques such as videos or role-playing, it is preferable to let the group know right from the start how the focus group interaction will be structured. This can relieve tensions and anxiety, and so encourage more open discussion. And, while it is important for the moderator to maintain overall control of the content of the discussion, once the objectives and format have been explained, discussion will be more spontaneous and free-flowing if the group members themselves are allowed to set the pace and general structure of their responses. The moderator thus has a significant influence on the group and often needs to exert control in order to elicit the desired range and depth of opinions. Yet the moderator must also be reasonably open and relaxed in allowing the group to establish its own style and pace and not feel overly manipulated. Chapter six will look more closely at the role of the moderator and how that individual can affect the quality of the focus group discussion.

Although the influences exerted by the moderator and other factors outside the group can be significant, the success of the methodology ultimately depends on the fact that the focus group is a *group*. This chapter has provided a brief look at how groups form and interact so that those utilizing the focus group technique can better understand and use the phenomenon of group process to their advantage. After all, it is because of what happens during the group process that this type of interview was first recognized as a useful way to gather qualitative research data. The next chapter will provide some background information on how the method was developed and discuss some examples of how it has been successfully used by researchers and organizations in a variety of settings.

REFERENCES

1. Shaw ME. Group dynamics: the psychology of small group behavior. 3rd ed. New York: McGraw-Hill, 1981:8.
2. Hare AP. Handbook of small group research. 2nd ed. New York: The Free Press, 1976:16.
3. Gordon W, Langmaid R. Qualitative market research: a practitioner's and buyer's guide. Aldershot, England: Gower, c1988.
4. Tuckman B. Developmental sequences in small groups. Psych Bull 1965; 63:384–99.
5. Gordon, op. cit., 41.
6. *Ibid.*, 37.

3

DEVELOPMENT AND USAGE OF THE FOCUS GROUP TECHNIQUE

The development and use of the methodology now known as the focus group has had a lengthy and varied history. Although it was first recognized as a useful data gathering technique among social scientists, this group of professionals did not immediately embrace the method in their research. Rather it was in the field of marketing where focus group interviews first became popularized and introduced to a large number of people. Only later did the social science community rediscover the usefulness of the method, during the 1960s and '70s. Since then, a growing number of researchers have recognized its value, and focus group interviews have become a well-established part of formal and informal research projects.

The interview technique from which today's focus group developed was first used some seventy years ago, with one of the earliest accounts documented by Bogardus in 1926 [1]. While organizing groups of school boys to talk about their ideas, Bogardus recognized the value of the creative discussion that developed among the group participants. He described the characteristics that are unique to group discussions and are so highly valued in today's focus groups: how a statement from one member starts a train of thought in others; how people develop new points of view that had not previously occurred to them; and how people draw on their own experience in defending their views when others in the group express contradictory views. None of these insights, he believed, were possible in the individual interview. By 1930, many social scientists had become dissatisfied with the traditional methods of interviewing individuals to gather information. Of great concern were the predetermined, highly-structured questions routinely used in interviews at that time. The questions and techniques limited the responses of those being questioned and allowed too much influence by the interviewer [2]. The concept of a more open-ended, nondirective interview was appealing, since it allowed respondents to assume more control over the content and direction of the discussion and thus bring out more of what were their own ideas and concerns rather than what was on the interviewer's mind.

Little use of the group interview seems to have been made, however, until the 1940s, when the sociologist Paul Lazarsfeld began to utilize group interviewing during the Second World War. His work on testing responses to radio morale programs attracted the interest of another sociologist, Robert Merton, who subsequently joined with Lazarsfeld to further develop the technique [3]. Merton went on to use the technique extensively and described both the procedures and its rationale in 1946 in the *American Journal of Sociology* [4]. Ten years later the authors published the first manual describing focused interviews, including a chapter devoted to the use of the technique with groups. This book still stands as the classic work on group interviewing [5].

In spite of this early development within the field of sociology, the technique does not seem to have been widely utilized by social scientists in the following years and Merton's book was never widely sold. Focus groups, however, did grow in popularity among another group of professionals. In the 1960s, the technique was enthusiastically adopted by the advertising and marketing worlds who used it to gather customer-related data. Knowing that the decision to purchase a product depends not only on satisfaction with the actual product, but just as importantly on deeper psychological factors, private industry could clearly benefit by understanding and utilizing those factors to enhance their products' image or value. It is no wonder then that the business world turned to qualitative research methods such as focus groups. These methods could provide them with the types of insight into the underlying emotional processes which determine human behavior that would not be possible with quantitative measures [6]. Focus group interviewing was quickly seen as a useful strategy in finding out what would sell and how it might best be sold, simply by listening, under controlled interview conditions, to the people who would be doing the buying. As a technique the focus group produced believable results at a reasonable cost; it could save businesses from making costly mistakes in the marketplace.

The world of marketing may originally have been attracted to the focus group because early users of the technique came from the field of communications research and frequently used items such as story boards and movies as "stimulus material" [7]. Such methods were easily adapted by market researchers to assess how consumers might respond to various products and services. By 1980, focus groups were the predominant method for conducting qualitative research in the field of marketing. A study published at that time showed that focus groups were the most popular technique for evaluating television commercials among users of this type of advertising [8]. In subsequent years focus group interviews have been utilized by lawyers to assess how jurors might react to the theory of a case [9]; and by banks to learn about customer needs, improve their public image, and boost profits [10]. Certified public accountants have used the information from focus groups to reduce client turnover and increase referrals [11], while hospitals have improved their billing practices through what they learned from these types of discussions [12]. Indeed, a whole range of business concerns have made use of the focus group as they try to understand how their consumers regard their products and services. And, for similar reasons, the technique has become popular in the field of politics. Both individual candidates and parties routinely employ focus groups to identify issues of concern to various voter groups and to evaluate public impressions of themselves and their organization. The technique has in fact become the heart of modern political research and is heavily used to modulate and direct policies and actions on the individual and party level. As witness to the technique's widening appeal, a second edition of Merton's book was published in 1990 [13].

TABLE 3–1

FOCUS GROUP USERS

- Advertising
- Anthropology
- Banking
- Health Care
- Librarianship
- Marketing
- Politics
- Teaching

While much of the use of focus groups has centered on understanding the customer, many businesses, as well as other types of organizations in the public and private sectors, have also made use of the technique in dealing with issues concerning personnel. Employee feedback elicited through this method can be extremely valuable to management, because it provides them with a window on how staff see the organization, its policies, and their own place in the larger unit.

Focus groups have been used to learn how to improve job performance, to develop employee benefit packages, to help both terminated and continuing staff cope with layoffs, and generally improve employee-employer relations. The technique has been particularly useful in the area of staff development because of its effectiveness in evaluating training programs and materials [14]. While questionnaires and written class evaluations may show that attendees approve strongly of a particular program or trainer, they will not reveal the long term success of the training: has it improved job-related performance? Can employees in fact use the methods taught in the class? Qualitative methods, however, can provide exactly this type of information, through eliciting the actual experiences and feelings of those who have attended the training sessions.

Back to Social Sciences: As the business world was expanding its use of focus group interviewing, researchers and others in the field of social science began to turn back to qualitative methods. In part this was because of a desire to better understand the human experience, which numbers alone could not provide [15]. One major impetus behind this return to techniques such as the focus group was the growing need for evaluating social programs. Although not usually motivated by profit, as in the world of commercial marketing, social and political organizations do have a vested interest in "marketing" their own products: the services and information they provide. The cost-conscious environment of the 1970s and '80s meant that even these programs were now being held more strictly accountable for the resources they used. Moreover, an increasingly sophisticated clientele was simultaneously demanding better, more effective service. Hence, service organizations were being faced with the need not only to document what they were doing but also to demonstrate the impact their services really had. Just as marketing and advertising staff understood the importance of knowing their customers, service organizations began to realize that they too could benefit from a better understanding of their clients' needs.

Of all social service areas, the health care field in particular became increasingly aware of the potential role of their consumers in improving the quality of the services they used. Focus groups are not new to health care providers; the literature shows many examples of the technique being used to understand attitudes and behavior toward a wide variety of health related issues. Basch, in one of the more comprehensive discussions of the technique in health care, provides many examples, including projects to study teenage smoking, high blood pressure in hypertensives, and contraceptive use in different cultures [16]. His own use of the focus group method was to study the opinions and feelings of young people toward traffic safety to identify fears that prevent safety conscious behavior and beliefs that influence their perceptions and actions. Understanding the perceptions, beliefs, and motivations of patients has been a critical factor in the development of health education programs for some time. In this new environment, however, patients, or consumers, not only helped in developing a more successful health intervention, they also began to play a role in defining the quality of those interventions. Just as in the business world, health care services in the late 1970s began to draw on the concepts of quality assurance to determine if standards were being met. While the traditional approach emphasized the use of data gathered retroactively in order to determine where mistakes were made, the newer approach to total quality management focused on a continuous review of outcomes. Consumers had an important role in determining how the success of those outcomes should be judged [17]. In the new paradigm, quality would be defined through a partnership of provider and consumer, where service goals (outcomes) reflected both the knowledge and experience of providers and the expectations and values of consumers. What better way to determine consumer views than through a qualitative approach such as the focus group?

Focus groups have been used by a wide range of health service providers, including hospitals, clinics, home care, and nursing services. Examples in the literature document the success of the technique in many settings and with a wide range of patients. It has been used to understand issues involved with children's health awareness to the needs of those caring for Alzheimer patients. The abundance of such literature clearly demonstrates the appeal of the focus group discussion among all sorts of organizations as a way of gaining a better understanding of those whom the organization serves. Although some library managers may have recognized the value of the technique and used it within their institutions, there is little mention of such instances in the library literature before the 1980s. Those examples that have been documented clearly show the adaptability of the method to library situations. Before examining the factors involved in running focus groups, it will therefore be helpful to review some of the documented examples of this technique within the library setting. The cases reviewed in chapter four illustrate the usefulness of the focus group, in a wide variety of projects, in exploring the needs and attitudes of library patrons and staff.

REFERENCES

1. Bogardus ES. The group interview. J Appl Soc 1926;10(4):372–382.
2. Krueger RA. Focus groups: a practical guide for applied research. 2nd ed. Thousand Oaks, CA: Sage Publications, 1994:7.
3. Merton RK. The focused interview and focus groups: continuities and discontinuities. Publ Opin Q 1987 Win;51(4):550–66.
4. Merton RK, Kendall PL. The focused interview. Amer J Sociol 1946;51:541–57.
5. Merton RK, Fiske M, Kendall, PL. The focused interview. New York: The Free Press, 1956.
6. Folch-Lyon E, Trost JF. Conducting focus group sessions. Stud Fam Plann 1981 Dec;12(12):443–9.
7. Morgan DL. Focus groups as qualitative research. Newbury Park, CA: Sage Publications, 1988:12.
8. Coe BJ, MacLachlan JH. How major TV advertisers evaluate commercials. J Adv Res 1980;20(6):51–4.
9. Clark LJ. Focus groups. Legal Asst Today 1993 Jul/Aug;10(6):148–151.
10. Green A. Bank marketers focus on focus groups. Bankers Monthly 1990 Apr;107(4):32–5.
11. Karns D, Roehm HA, Castellano JF, Moore GB. Using focus groups to monitor clients' views. J Accountancy 1988 Oct;166(4):148–52.
12. Bernstein L, Harris J, Meloy R. Focus groups improve billing practices, patient relations. Healthcare Financial Man 1989 May;43(5):57–60.
13. Merton RK, Fiske M, Kendall PL. The focused interview: a manual of problems and procedures. 2nd ed. New York: Free Press, 1990.
14. Erkut S, Fields JP. Focus groups to the rescue. Train Dev J 1987 Oct;41(10):74–6.
15. Krueger RA. Focus groups: a practical guide for applied research. Newbury Park, CA: Sage, 1988:21.
16. Basch CE. Focus group interview: an underutilized research technique for improving theory and practice in health education. Health Ed Q 1987 Win;14(4):411–48.
17. Peters DA. Improving quality requires consumer input: using focus groups. J Nurs Care Qual 1993 Jan;7(2):34–41.

4

FOCUS GROUPS IN THE LIBRARY SETTING

Libraries, just like other service organizations in the early 1980s, began to discover that the focus group could be a convenient new methodology for studying user needs. There are descriptions in the library literature of some of these first uses of group discussions with clientele: to gain insight into how the library's services and collections are perceived, to generate ideas for improvements, and to determine future directions. The technique gained popularity in the next decade, and written accounts increased throughout the '90s. Apart from its use by various types of libraries, the focus group interview was also utilized by organizations and businesses that serve libraries. Some of the cases described here used it as a self-contained method while others combined the technique with other, quantitative measures; all found it a reliable way of gathering information.

One of the earliest cases reported, by Scharf and Ward, describes the use of focus groups by the library at the University of Central Florida [1]. Library staff conducted group discussions in the spring of 1985 to obtain student perceptions of the library to help in planning and setting priorities for programs that would improve library services. The results were very helpful and some of the knowledge gained by the discussions was put into immediate effect. Solutions to concerns such as the need for more quiet space and for duplicate copies of certain heavily used reference tools, which were mentioned by a large number of the participants, were quickly implemented. Moreover, the project convinced the library that focus groups could be used as an efficient and cost effective research methodology for exploring many user-related issues.

In a different setting, the focus group method was also successfully used to understand better the role of a special library and its value to the parent organization. A graduate student and faculty members from the University of Minnesota, School of Journalism and Mass Communication, conducted focus group interviews in 1986 with the staff of a metropolitan daily newspaper [2]. Separate groups of editorial staff and news library staff were convened and, in each case, information from the focus groups was used to develop research surveys for further study. What the study found was that the library's contributions, both in resources and services, are central to the newsmaking mission of the newspaper, yet usually go unrecognized in studies of how news is made. The study is a good example of the use of a qualitative method to help design meaningful questions for a quantitative survey.

In contrast to these relatively few accounts of library focus groups reported in the 1980s, many more examples from library settings are found in the literature starting in 1990. A search of the LISA, Library Literature, and ERIC databases in mid-1997, identified over ninety references, dating from 1990 through 1997, to examples of libraries, library organizations, or library-related businesses using the methodology. By far the largest population utilizing focus groups was in the academic setting. Forty reports were found from college and university libraries that described a variety of uses, both general and specific: assessment of library services, collections, instructional programs, and organizational structure; strategic planning; understanding the information seeking behaviors of users; reactions to electronic services; patterns of Internet use; and undergraduate use of the library for research. Although most applications were used to investigate patron attitudes and needs, several projects involved library staff as the focus, looking at performance, attitude toward the job, and effects of changes to the organizational structure.

While college and university libraries accounted for the highest use of focus group discussions in the literature, some references highlighted the technique in other types of libraries. Twenty four reports were found that involved public libraries and included a variety of topics: developing methods for evaluating supervisors; studying patron use of the Internet; improving the library's business sources; evaluating services for children and youths; examining reciprocal borrowing patterns within a library system; evaluating the need for expanded reference services for adult students (in conjunction with academic libraries); and determining continuing education needs of the library's staff. A total of seven school library projects were identified in this same time period. These included the use of focus groups with children to study their use of computers in the library and to gather their ideas in planning a new library, and an investigation of the role of the library media program in the school's instructional program. The literature search also identified six examples of use by state libraries: to develop a long range plan for youth services and guidelines for bookmobiles; to evaluate literacy programs, library buildings, and a statewide library continuing education plan. Finally, five articles described the use of focus group projects in special libraries: law, medical, and corporate.

The remaining references were to projects in which the technique was used by a variety of vendors of library products and services, and library-related organizations.

TABLE 4–1

LIBRARY TOPICS FOR FOCUS GROUP DISCUSSIONS

- Assessment of library collections
- Continuing education needs of staff
- Effects of organizational change on staff
- Patterns of Internet use by patrons
- Strategic planning
- Patron evaluation of library services
- Information seeking behavior of patrons
- Patron reaction to new services
- Instructional program evaluation

Clearly the focus group technique has become an important tool for use in the library. As in other institutions, the method has been used either alone or in conjunction with other research methods. In one instance, focus groups were used at Purdue University within the library system to expand on information gathered by a survey [3]. The survey had been administered to students and faculty to learn about how they used the campus libraries and their attitudes toward library collections, facilities, and training classes. Although the survey had included some open-ended questions, this technique had not produced enough information to be truly useful for library staff. Several student focus groups were then conducted and analysis revealed concerns that had not been evident from the survey responses and were valuable to the library administration. Moreover, as is often the case, the discussions brought out topics that had not been included in the original set of questions. In this instance, two issues emerged: one concerned a new computerized reference system. Students said they found the system useful but unanimously agreed that more terminals were needed to provide easier access to the system. The other issue concerned how students learn to use the library; here a strong feeling emerged that current levels of instruction were inadequate. Since both issues were obviously important to the first group, the moderator introduced them into subsequent groups, thereby gaining additional insight into these important student concerns.

Another example of a combined approach was at Linfield College in Oregon, where library staff investigated the attitudes and skills of undergraduates in conducting library research [4]. The project used both focus groups and individual interviews, and found each methodology to be useful. Several benefits of focus groups emerged. In the groups, participants interacted largely with one another with little input needed from the moderator. Themes emerged as students responded to one another's comments, finding they had many experiences in common. The moderator was thus able to step back from the discussion and this resulted in less of an emotional and intellectual drain on the librarian, and greater freedom of discussion within the group. In the individual interviews, this was not the case. The moderator worked hard to draw out students and in one case found that the interviewee was quite concerned that her opinions might not be "correct" because there were none of her peers there to validate them. Another major benefit of the focus groups was the time spent to gather the information. Only three hours were needed to conduct two groups, involving twelve students, whereas each individual interview required an hour. Overall the library staff felt that the project had been a success and that they learned some valuable information about how students use library resources. They were especially pleased with the focus group process. In this instance, the methodology had proved to be quick and effective, and was seen as a viable and less time-consuming complement to other methodologies.

Librarians as Participants: At the same time that librarians were beginning to realize the value of the focus group technique, some of the research and commercial organizations that provide services and products to libraries were also utilizing the technique to help them develop better products. In perhaps the first published report of focus groups involving libraries, staff at the OCLC Research Department described their use of the technique as one method of determining the features needed for a successful subject retrieval system [5]. The groups included both patrons and librarians from public, school, special, college, and university/research libraries. Their discussions provided OCLC with valuable insight into library users' perceptions, expectations and criteria for success when accessing subjects. As a result, the decision was made to conduct further research and testing to determine exactly which of the features mentioned by the groups would be practical and cost effective to build into a subject retrieval system. In a related project, focus groups were again utilized by OCLC researchers in evaluating needs and perceptions of library users regarding online public access catalogs, or OPACs [6]. The groups involved both users and non-users of OPACs, including patrons and library staff in public, federal, and university libraries. The group discussions were used to further explore information gathered from questionnaires, thus personalizing and further defining information obtained from a quantitative study. In each instance, information from the focus groups eventually affected the design and content of the OCLC products and programs.

In a somewhat different situation, several major American publishers have used librarians in focus groups to better understand the library market. These groups have provided publishers with valuable information on how librarians select and purchase books for their libraries, as well as their reactions to new manuscripts and products, and to potential marketing and development strategies [7]. This type of relationship between publishers and working librarians is in fact an ongoing one because publishers frequently use librarians as advisory board members; focus groups are seen as just another method of listening to the customer.

As a mark of the growing usefulness of focus group interviewing to libraries, Wagner and Mahmoodi developed a brief manual, specifically aimed at libraries, which was published in 1994 by the Continuing Library Education Network and Exchange Round Table of the American Library Association [8]. The manual delineates responsibilities for those involved with the group; provides advice on the preparation, execution, and follow-up of the actual discussion; and includes some useful examples of questions for various library settings. A particularly valuable section in this manual is the description of the attributes needed for each member of the focus group team: moderator, recorder, and optional observer. Included here are skills such as the ability to pose open-ended questions, to listen carefully, and to encourage people to speak, as well as the importance of liking people. All these attributes point to the fact that many librarians, especially those experienced in public service delivery, already possess some of the key skills needed to successfully use this technique.

Use in Health Sciences Libraries: While university and some types of special libraries have begun to conduct focus groups for a variety of reasons, very little use by health sciences libraries is recorded in the literature. One of the first cases described is that by Robbins and Holst at Columbia Hospital in Milwaukee, Wisconsin, in 1990 [9]. This project included three focus groups, composed of physicians, other clinical personnel, and non-clinical personnel, who represented many departments within the hospital. The moderator was a library intern who was unknown to group participants. In spite of the problem of poor attendance, the information gathered from the groups provided library staff with a good view of how users saw the library, and suggested to library staff some new ideas, including how to better publicize services. The discussions also shed light on some misconceptions about the library, including its photocopying capabilities and reprint collections. Clearly satisfied with the technique, the library found practical applications for the information generated: data were used in a subsequent library renovation plan and in a grant proposal to acquire new search equipment.

A second example from the library of the University of Missouri, Columbia, illustrates the use of focus groups for a more specific purpose. Here the technique was used to evaluate the library's current services and bibliographic training program as they pertained to the newly implemented problem-based learning curriculum in the School of Medicine [10]. This project was judged to be successful because several areas were identified where services could be improved. One of the outcomes was development of a new orientation for first-year students, which included much more hands-on time. A second was the creation of an information notebook for the students, to act as a survival guide for using library resources. Study outcomes also suggested the provision of more extensive training courses for electronic information resources, and that some traditional library services, including circulation and reserves, should be re-evaluated. Library staff also felt that further discussion groups could serve as a good method of building and sustaining public relations with the School of Medicine.

The focus group technique has been successfully used within the National Network of Libraries of Medicine by two Regional Medical Libraries (RMLs). The projects for both libraries were undertaken as part of their contractual agreements with the National Library of Medicine, to assess the information needs of health professionals within their region. In the Pacific Southwest (PS) Region, the UCLA Louise Darling Biomedical Library held discussions with each of six different health professional groups: nurses, dentists, pharmacologists, clinical psychologists, rural hospital administrators, and veterinarians. Each group was led by a librarian staff member of PSRML, with a second member acting as recorder/observer. Other than the discussion with administrators, each group was made up of practitioners, faculty, and students, in order to gain varied perspectives on the profession's information needs. The focus group technique revealed extremely useful factors specific to each health professional group concerning their information usage. For example, dentists identified a need for information that is more product-oriented and less of a need for the large body of reference resources [11]. Clinical psychologists described a varied need for information drawn from psychology, medicine, business, etc., and hence the importance of access to a large variety of databases. Moreover, they felt that their information needs were changing with respect to the influence of managed care on their practices [12]. RML staff reported that these focus groups were an extremely positive experience. Participants frequently expressed gratitude, after the discussions, for the opportunity to be heard by the National Library of Medicine. They also felt they had benefited from the chance to focus their own thinking on how they and their students need and utilize information, and to learn from one another. This phenomenon has in fact been noted in other focus group projects where participants reported that discussions had influenced subsequent thinking and behavior [13]. Because of the success of the technique, the RML in California has incorporated focus group discussions into its present contract, in order to assess a variety of information needs, including Internet use by health professionals.

A different approach was used in the Midcontinental Region, where the University of Nebraska McGoogan Library of Medicine engaged a marketing firm to conduct focus groups to determine information needs, both met and unmet, of health care professionals in the region [14]. Here participants were again divided by health profession but were in some cases further broken down into separate groupings for clinical and academic users or for urban and rural users. A total of fourteen group discussions was conducted, including allied health professionals, nurses, dentists, physicians, pharmacists, residents, hospital administrators, and medical librarians. As in the California RML project, the Regional Medical Library in Nebraska used the same "script" of questions with each succeeding group, so that comparisons could be made between the different professions. The project resulted in a communication plan for the RML to improve service to its customers that included many practical aspects. For example, comments from many of the groups on health professionals' use of Grateful Med revealed the difficulties end-user searchers have with understanding and using *Medical Subject Headings* (MeSH). Moreover, RML staff felt that in general they had gained important insight into the clients they serve, which will help them in planning targeted programs and in carrying out their own quality improvement activities.

The focus group technique proved to be extremely valuable in the two regions; important insights were gained into the needs of the various health professional groups, their approach to information, and the problems they encountered. Information gathered from the groups in both areas was used to target future RML programs and services and to be more responsive to regional needs. In the Pacific Southwest Region project, for example, staff learned about the important role that pharmacists play in providing information to other health care professionals in many rural and underserved hospitals that have no library staff. This resulted both in a greater effort to include this group in training classes provided during PSRML outreach visits and in making the pharmacist the initial contact at future outreach sites. Moreover, by publishing the results of the focus group discussions in regional newsletters, the RMLs were able to share their insight with other health sciences libraries who serve the same groups of users.

Clearly the focus group technique can be a useful tool for the health sciences library to gain a better understanding of user needs and approaches to information. Hospital libraries may find the technique especially helpful in fulfilling one of the requirements for hospital accreditation, as determined by the Joint Commission on the Accreditation of Health Care Organizations (JCAHO) [15]. In 1993, these standards were completely revised for all departments within the hospital or other health care institution and expectations for library services changed significantly. With an overall emphasis on individual functions important to patient care, one of the revised standards for information management within the hospital specifies the need to regularly assess user needs. The focus group technique appears to be a relatively easy and cost-effective method to employ for this type of assessment.

Survey of Health Sciences Library Use: A brief survey was conducted in the fall of 1995, to ascertain the level of knowledge about focus group interviewing, and how the technique has been utilized among these types of libraries to supplement the few extant examples related to health sciences libraries. A survey questionnaire was sent to all 132 members of the Association of Academic Health Sciences Library Directors (AAHSLD) and to 210 non-academic health sciences libraries, mostly in hospitals. Information about these non-academic libraries was provided by the RMLs throughout the country. Of the 342 surveys sent out, 176 were returned, a response rate of 51%. Of the responses returned, 85 were from academic libraries and 91 were from non-academic libraries.

Results showed that among the large, academic institutions, thirty libraries (35%) had used the technique, while only thirteen (14%) of the smaller libraries had, making an overall total of forty-three libraries (24%) who had used focus groups. In a large majority of these libraries (70%), the discussion was led by a librarian on staff. Only fourteen libraries used someone outside the organization to lead the group and of these, nine used a professional moderator. All libraries that had used focus groups felt the results were useful, with three qualifying this as "somewhat useful." None of the libraries said that the results were not useful, indicating that they learned at least something from the discussion. Only one library that had used focus groups indicated that it would not use the technique again. Interestingly, this particular library had used a professional moderator and felt that the individual had no real knowledge of the topic; hence the dissatisfaction with the process. This illustrates the significance of using a moderator who has a good understanding of the topic under discussion. Successful focus groups need moderators who not only have experience with the technique, but who have sufficient knowledge of the environment in which the discussion will take place. If libraries do choose an outside professional moderator, it is critical that library staff work closely with this individual before the actual groups meet.

The survey revealed a wide variety of applications in the health sciences library environment. Apart from the more general use as a tool in strategic or long-range planning, or to learn about the information needs of specific groups of users (*e.g.*, faculty, rural health practitioners) focus group discussions were also utilized for very specific purposes. These included: evaluation of individual library programs (*e.g.*, circuit librarian program); revision of the library's collection development policy; development of a mission statement for the library; determination of the support services needed for computers added to the library; and a study of users' access to electronic publications. And while most libraries conducted focus groups to learn more about the needs of their users, some used the technique to focus on their own staff. One library held group discussions with reference desk staff to better understand their anxieties and sources of pressure; another used the process to study the changes and transitions associated with a major automation project in the library to help staff deal more successfully with those changes.

Among those libraries that had not used focus groups, the most frequently cited reason given by non-academic libraries was lack of familiarity with the technique, followed by lack of need. Among the academic libraries this order was reversed. Several libraries of both types cited lack of resources to hire a professional moderator as their reason for non-utilization. However, almost every library, both academic and non-academic, indicated that it would be willing to use focus groups in the future. It seems obvious that there is a great deal of interest in this technique and libraries who have used their own staff to conduct focus groups have been satisfied with the results. Given the growing need for some method of assessing user needs that can easily be repeated in a cost-effective manner, and the skills of many librarians experienced in public service techniques, the focus group method is clearly one that libraries might readily adopt for their needs.

Added Benefits: The examples given here of using focus groups in the library indicate the usefulness of this technique in understanding more about library users' needs and perceptions. The knowledge gained has been used to implement new and improved services, or simply to change the way things have been done in the past to reflect current needs. Some of those conducting focus groups, however, have realized other, unexpected benefits from the library's participation in this activity. The act of consulting users and listening to their needs has proved to be a useful exercise in public relations as in the University of Missouri example [16]. At the University of Central Florida, the fact that the library was conducting user research was mentioned in the university's publications, bringing positive attention to the library [17]. A focus group project conducted jointly by libraries at UCLA and the University of California, Berkeley, to develop new services for undergraduates was similarly useful beyond the immediate goals of the project [18]. Librarians found the results of the discussions in the University of California study to be very revealing of students' lack of knowledge about the library and how to best use its resources for research. Partly in response to these findings, an information literacy survey was subsequently conducted, which again highlighted students' inability to conduct effective library research. Being able to cite these results in discussions with faculty members and teaching assistants proved a strong argument for integrating research skills into the curriculum.

While librarians are relatively new to the use of the focus group discussion, they have clearly benefited from this technique in very practical ways. As the literature shows, focus groups have been successfully used in assessing user needs and developing more responsive services, in public, special, state, and academic settings [19]. Libraries that have used focus groups, in most cases, have conducted the discussions themselves and have been pleased with the results. With a limited budget and lack of time for extensive research, this method is very appealing to smaller libraries. The remainder of this book is devoted to a consideration of the factors involved in successfully using focus group discussions in the library setting.

REFERENCES

1. Scharf MK, Ward J. A library research application of focus group interviews. In: Energies for transition. The Association of College and Research Libraries' National Conference. Chicago: The Association, 1986:191–3.
2. Ward J, Hansen KA, McLeod DM. The news library's contribution to newsmaking. Spec Libr 1988 Spring; 79(2):143–7.
3. Widdows R, Hensler TA, Wyncott MH. The focus group interview: a method for assessing users' evaluation of library service. Col & Res Libr 1991 July; 52:352–9.
4. Valentine B. Undergraduate research behavior: using focus groups to generate theory. J Acad Libr 1993 Nov; 19(5):300–4.
5. Kaske NK, Sanders NP. On-line subject access: the human side of the problem. RQ 1980 Fall; 19:52–8.
6. Markey K. Online catalog use: results of surveys and focus group interviews in several libraries. v.2. Dublin, OH: Online Computer Library Center, Inc., 1983. (ERIC ED231403)
7. Burroughs R. Book publishers focus on librarian focus groups. Libr J 1989 Mar 15; 114(5):48–9.
8. Wagner MM, Mahmoodi SH. A focus group interview manual. New York: American Library Association, Continuing Library Education Network and Exchange Round Table, 1994.
9. Robbins K, Holst R. Hospital library evaluation using focus group interviews. Bull Med Libr Assoc 1990 July;78(3):311–3.
10. Canning CS, Edwards AJ, Meadows SE. Using focus groups to evaluate library services in a problem-based curriculum. Med Ref Serv Q 1995 Fall;143(3):75–81.
11. Glitz B. PSRML focus group discussion targets dentistry. Latitudes 1994 Mar/Apr;3(2):1–3.
12. Glitz B. PSRML focus group on psychology. Latitudes 1994 Sep/Oct; 3(5):1–2.

13. Swenson JD, Griswold WF, Kleiber PB. Focus groups: method of inquiry / intervention. Small Group Res 1992 Nov;23(4):459–74.
14. Mullaly-Quijas P, Ward DH, Woelfl N. Using focus groups to discover health professionals' information needs: a regional marketing study. Bull Med Libr Assoc 1994 July;82(3):305–11.
15. 1994 Accreditation Manual for Hospitals. Vol. 1. Standards. Oakbrook Terrace, IL: Joint Commission on the Accreditation of Health Care Organizations, 1993.
16. Canning, op. cit.
17. Scharf, op. cit.
18. Meltzer E, Maughan PD, Fry TK. Undergraduate in focus: can student input lead to new directions in planning undergraduate library services? Libr Trends 1995 Fall;44(2):400–22.
19. Connaway LS. Focus group interviews: a data collection methodology for decision making. Libr Admin & Man 1996 Fall;10(4):231–9.

5

STRENGTHS AND WEAKNESSES: WHEN SHOULD THE FOCUS GROUP BE USED

The previous chapters of this book have provided some background information on how and why the focus group interview technique works as a qualitative research method. The many examples, both published and unpublished, of its use among commercial, research, and service organizations, attest to its wide applicability for data gathering. Those contemplating the use of the technique, however, need to understand that like any other research method, it can have drawbacks. Before going on to describe the various factors in running focus group projects, it will be helpful, therefore, to review here the strengths and weaknesses of the focus group as a research methodology for librarians. Potential users should consider these factors in light of their own needs, before investing in the time and effort needed to conduct a focus group project.

Focus Group Strengths: Perhaps the focus group's greatest strength is that it draws on the natural inclinations of people to be sociable. Human beings like to interact with one another and tend to make decisions after discussion and listening to others. The focus group setting takes advantage of this and with its relatively "natural" environment, encourages more openness and candor in the participants' responses than other techniques [1]. Such a setting tends to lessen individual anxiety and encourage fuller participation. Hearing other people speak about similar experiences and feelings can help participants overcome anxiety or hesitation to offer their own views and thoughts to the discussion. This can be especially useful, for example, when dealing with populations who may be put off by lengthy questionnaires or individual interviews that might appear to be overly time-consuming, detailed, or even irrelevant to their own needs and interests. Potential users should therefore ask themselves: can I learn what I need to know from a frank discussion of this subject?

```
┌─────────────────────────────────────────────────────┐
│                     TABLE 5–1                        │
│                                                      │
│   FOCUS GROUPS—THE ADVANTAGES FOR LIBRARY MANAGERS   │
│        • Projects can be conducted quickly           │
│        • Expenses can be moderate                    │
│        • In-house staff can be utilized              │
│        • Allows face-to-face contact with users      │
│        • Methodology has a wide range of uses        │
│        • Results are easily understandable           │
│        • Methodology is flexible and simple          │
│                                                      │
└─────────────────────────────────────────────────────┘
```

On a practical level, a second major advantage of focus groups is that they can be conducted relatively quickly and at moderate expense, especially compared with other methods of data collection. Surveys, for example, can take months to prepare, distribute, collect, and analyze. Yet in the same time it takes to conduct one individual interview, the focus group can gather a range of informative opinions from many individuals. One study of undergraduate research behavior found that each individual interview took about one hour to complete, whereas two focus groups, involving twelve students, were completed within a total of four hours [2]. In fact, the entire focus group process: organizing, conducting, and analyzing, can be completed in as little as a few weeks [3].

For the library using its own staff to conduct the focus groups, speed and simplicity in information accumulation are especially important, given the fact that the same staff will almost certainly be expected to carry on with their regular duties. Yet this ability to utilize in-house staff for much if not all of the focus group project is a third major advantage. Although there is some disagreement in the literature about the use of an organization's own staff to lead the discussion, many have done so successfully, reasoning that in-house staff have a better understanding of the underlying issues than any outsider could have. While it is critical that insiders refrain from attempting to impose their own ideas and prejudices on the group, they often can more quickly and easily lead the group to the important points of the group interview and more effectively interpret the information that is obtained. Careful selection of appropriate staff to lead a discussion can reduce the danger of undue moderator influence. Utilizing a librarian who is not directly affected by the outcome of the discussions, for example, choosing an individual from technical services to lead a group on public service issues, can help assure neutrality in the way the discussion is led. From a budget point of view, the use of library staff to conduct the sessions can be an important consideration, given the high costs of using professional moderators.

Whoever ultimately leads the discussion, the ability to engage in a face-to-face interaction with those whose opinions are sought is a fifth major advantage of the focus group methodology [4]. Such interaction allows both the moderator and the other participants to ask for clarification or more information when a response is unclear or incomplete at any point in the discussion. It is much harder to do this type of probing on a written survey when responses must be predicted beforehand or the survey re-written to accommodate additional responses. The face-to-face characteristics of the focus group argue strongly for having library staff participate in the discussion since they can hear directly what their patrons think and immediately relate it to their own library environment.

Another major benefit of the focus group is that the methodology can be less intimidating than other forms of data collection. This is especially important if those conducting the project are not trained in research methodologies. The construction and analysis of a lengthy questionnaire can appear overwhelming, raising concerns about the precise wording of questions and the need to understand statistical concepts. While it is equally important to construct good questions for a focus group, and ask them in a logical order, there is some comfort for the novice researcher in the flexibility of this methodology. The ability to adapt or rephrase the questions during the actual discussion to suit the particular group, without changing their actual meaning, makes the focus group technique more accommodating to inexperienced researchers.

As suggested by the considerations above, as well as being relatively simple and inexpensive the focus group methodology is also flexible and extremely open-ended. The format allows for easy modification during a project if this is found to improve the quality or amount of information gathered. Questions can be reworded or expanded; other questions can be added. And different groups or types of participants can be added to broaden the responses if needed [5]. Because of its very personalized format, it can be used to investigate many types of library questions and concerns and it is successful with all kinds of users. Many organizations have used focus groups with their own staff, to discuss a variety of management and personnel issues, though it is best in these circumstances to use a "neutral" moderator to encourage true openness in the discussion. Even here the moderator need not be a professional, but could perhaps be a librarian from a different section or from another library. The focus group is also a transportable methodology; since there is little in the way of equipment that is needed, groups can be brought together in various locations. Furthermore, multiple focus group discussions can produce results quickly. Several groups can be conducted within a few days, and because it is better to analyze the results soon after the actual discussion, while the experience is still fresh in the mind of the moderator, a report can be available often within a few weeks of the start of the project.

A final advantage of the method is that the results of focus groups can easily be presented in a manner that is readily understandable and usable. The normal method of presentation is through either a written or oral report. Since the report typically uses descriptive language, in lay terms, and often includes direct quotations, the individuals receiving the report do not need to cope with statistical terminology or complex graphs or charts to understand the results. For the institution sponsoring the focus group project, this has several benefits. Not only can results be quickly and easily understood, if needed, they can be transmitted to the rest of the staff without a great deal of interpretation. Furthermore, if the project has been set up to help identify the need for program or policy changes, the information can be readily utilized in making those changes. For example, if the project is conducted to evaluate the library's educational program and participants express an overwhelming need for more instruction in certain library tools, additional classes could be added to an existing schedule without any great disruption to other library services.

Disadvantages: While librarians can clearly take advantage of these strengths, focus groups do have some disadvantages and potential users must be aware of these factors if they are to utilize the technique to full advantage. Even when conducted by an experienced moderator, focus groups are not truly a "natural" setting for discussion. Talk among participants may be very different from spontaneous conversations between friends or colleagues. Because of this there is always some fear about the validity of what is said: do participants really say what they think or are they reacting to the more formal, research setting and saying what they think the organizers or even the other participants want them to say? [6]. A participant may "play up" to the audience or focus group leader with the hope of acceptance or personal advantage. Likewise, because the end results of a focus group depend heavily on the interaction of the group members, it may not follow that similar opinions and ideas about a topic would emerge from the same members on an individual basis. Clearly group behavior can differ greatly from individual behavior and the results of any discussion can be skewed by the influence of the group. While most people who attend focus groups are cooperative and willing to talk, some can be dominant, or unwilling to participate fully; ideas can become exaggerated or distorted, or alternatively, withheld because they might be seen as uninformed or foolish. All this can have a negative effect on the discussion and on the information gathered through the session. A single, unrepresentative or "rogue" focus group could mis-direct a library project and result in inappropriate or even counterproductive actions. Hence, it is important for most projects to use more than a single group discussion, especially when the data gathered will be used for the basis of important decision making.

In a related concern, moderators can also influence the outcome of a focus group through the amount of control they exert over the discussion and the behavior of the group. While a certain amount of freedom for the group is desirable at one level, in order to get full participation and honest responses, this same lack of control of how discussion progresses can lead to a corresponding lack of focus. If this happens, the information generated may not really be pertinent or useful to the overall project. Yet too much control by the moderator of the group's functioning can cause group members to respond inappropriately and again jeopardize the results of the discussion. Forceful moderators who exert too much control in order to keep the discussion moving may cause group members to respond more to them than to the topic of discussion. This can take the form of deliberately arguing with or challenging the moderator in order to save face, or it can lead to too much acquiescence or lack of personal expression in order to placate or please. Either way the results from such a focus group will not be a genuine reflection of how the group reacted to the subject of the discussion. The moderator must be very aware of the group atmosphere and distort the discussion as little as possible. Not all moderators will be equally adept in this exercise, and a library that is considering use of one of its own personnel as moderator must be totally realistic in its evaluation of this individual. If no librarian has the needed abilities, library management must assess its ability and desire to utilize a professional moderator.

Another potential drawback in using focus groups, especially when results will be used to change services or procedures, is a lack of perspective in analyzing and using the information gathered. There is danger in attempting to quantitate the results of a qualitative research technique. Too much over-generalizing of the results and applying them to library users as a whole can be misleading and even dangerous, especially if only one discussion group is held. Just because the group unanimously stated a particular opinion does not mean that all library users may agree with it. No single focus group is likely to reflect the range of opinions, interests, and involvements of the full patron population of a library. Results of a single discussion usually need to be further validated, either by conducting more focus groups or by using other techniques such as surveys. The single group is too small a sample and the focus group approach is too qualitative for use when making changes that might seriously affect services or result in large expenditures. Therefore, if statistical or quantitative information is ultimately needed, focus groups are only likely to be useful in helping to design a quantitative assessment; the focus group results cannot stand alone in this instance.

A final problem with using focus groups is raising false expectations among the participants. Inclusion in a focus group is a positive indication of the value of an individual's ideas to the library. Querying users about their satisfaction with a particular service and eliciting their suggestions for improvements can thus produce unintended results. Group participants may expect that significant changes will be made based on the needs they expressed or the suggestions they made, and if no changes (or different changes) result, individuals can feel they have been ignored, exploited, or betrayed. Because of this tendency, libraries need to make clear from the start that the purpose of the group is one of exploration and data gathering, not decision-making. Participants need to understand that other methods of input will be used, probably including further focus groups, and that factors such as budget and organizational goals will need to be considered. Providing this type of explanation early in the exercise is important for preserving good relations between the library and its users. On the other side, library managers must be willing to accept and act on the results of the research, even if the staff disagree with some of the opinions expressed.

Inappropriate Use of the Focus Group: The focus group is an excellent technique through which qualitative information can be gathered, and this is its primary goal and use. Library managers can employ the methodology to help them in a wide range of situations to plan and improve services and assess needs. There are, however, limitations to the technique that must be considered. Focus groups are not useful for the discussion of certain topics, nor can they solve a variety of problems which face the library. For example focus groups are unlikely to help library managers deal with an unproductive or uninformed staff member. Discussing inappropriate topics, or including participants with the wrong type of experience, can result in misleading or incomplete results. Most importantly, focus groups cannot generate statistically valid data. The approach is not quantitative, and its results must not be given quantitative significance. Inappropriate use of focus groups can lead to bad decision-making and may discourage other appropriate use of the technique.

TABLE 5–2

DON'T USE FOCUS GROUPS FOR . . .

- Personnel issues
- Conflict resolution
- Consensus building
- Attitude modification
- Numerical data gathering

Morgan emphasizes that focus groups should not be used to resolve conflicts, to build consensus, to make instant decisions, or to change attitudes [7]. Nor should they be used to improve communication between members of the group and those organizing the project. After all, communication within the focus group setting is intended to be one way, *i.e.*, from group members to moderator, since the main purpose is to listen and gather information. While all these issues can and often are accomplished in groups, these groups are of a very different nature: committees, working groups, support groups, etc. Because the reason for holding a focus group is to generate as much discussion as possible, deliberately trying to build any type of consensus clearly is at odds with its main purpose and ability. This can sometimes be a problem during a discussion, especially when a group is made up of individuals who are decision-makers and hold considerable power within their own organizations. The tendency to try to reach decisions or to encourage people to settle disputes is natural when people are brought together in a group and it is particularly hard for individuals who spend much of their time doing just that to change their attitudes and expectations. The moderator must be ready to contend with this, and to make sure that opposing viewpoints are heard and respected as valid. If necessary, the group should be reminded that the goal of the focus group is to gather opinions and information, and to hear every side of the question, not to get solutions. In a well prepared focus group, the way the questions are phrased should eliminate these problems. But a good moderator will understand that the tendency is always there.

Focus groups should also be avoided if the topic is not appropriate for the participants or if it just does not lend itself to discussion. Participants who have too little involvement in a particular area will not have much to add to the discussion. If the library, for example, is interested in reviewing a particular service to see if it is meeting user needs, it makes sense to invite those who have actually used the service. A focus group dealing with the availability of research journals would probably gain little from the inclusion of undergraduate students, while an inquiry into the availability of class reserve materials would be unlikely to benefit from the inclusion of senior graduate students or research staff. Mixing users and non-users can also have negative consequences. Non-users, since they have little to contribute, can get bored with the discussion and decide that focus groups are not appealing. The library may then lose potential participants for future groups in which these individuals could have made a useful contribution. On the other hand, non-users may be determined to speak, since that is what they came for, and can lead the group into digressions and so impact the whole discussion. In such a mix, the users who do have something to contribute, can also be affected, either by dominating the group with their opinions because others will not speak out, or by being discouraged to speak because of the lack of response from other members. All this can reduce the quality and fullness of the discussion, and the library may get little useful information from such a group. Screening potential members before the group is formed can help eliminate this problem and if a non-user does emerge in the discussion, a good moderator should be able to utilize their input for at least some of the discussion.

Whether or not people have experience with particular topics, some subjects are just not suitable for discussion by a group. While this is often true of very intimate topics, it is also true of some business matters about which the library may legitimately need information. Service issues that are directly controlled by the budget are one obvious area in which focus groups would not be appropriate. The group will not have the breadth of knowledge of the budget that is needed, nor will they understand and evaluate competing demands. Their only possible response would be to call for more or better services. Similarly, asking a group to discuss the need for more staffing at service points, or improved access to computer terminals would be a frustrating experience both for the library and the participants. No real group could be expected to ask for less service. Clearly library management must determine where dollars are spent, and it is unfair to raise user expectations of increases when the bottom line will not allow such changes.

Making decisions on journal cancellations, weeding specific items, or adding individual titles to the collection, is another area in which focus groups are not a good method for generating user input. Users can and do provide valuable information to the library in the collection development area. For example when new residency programs or academic subject areas call for expansion or changes to the collection, faculty or staff involved in these programs or disciplines can provide important information to the library. However, the focus group discussion would not be the best way to get this information. Health professionals and academic staff often have narrow interests even within the same department. A group discussion of these different needs might only set up a competitive atmosphere and would certainly not be an appealing topic to potential participants. Individual interviews would be more appropriate when the library wants this type of collection related advice. Where focus groups can be useful in the area of collection development is in exploring library users' attitudes and perceptions of, for example, the overall strengths and weaknesses of the collection, the types of formats included, and patterns of use. When in doubt, it might be useful to apply Morgan's commonsense method to determine appropriateness by asking "How easy will it be to generate a free-flowing and *productive* conversation on this topic?" (author's emphasis added) [8]. This simple technique can help the library make the best use of focus groups and avoid wasted time, frustration, and the potential for alienating library users.

While there are several instances when a focus group approach is not suitable, probably the most inappropriate use is in gathering numerical data from which to make projections. The focus group is an inherently qualitative instrument; it does not generate quantitative, statistical data. Library administrators often do need to get statistical information upon which to base management and other decisions, and these data clearly need to be as reliable and accurate as possible. But a focus group is not a reliable method for determining, for example, the percentage of users who feel the same way about an issue. For one thing, the group is much too small to produce a statistically significant number. Nor is it possible that the group selected will quantitatively mirror the target population; in fact the members are selected to give a range of opinions rather than to be typical of predominant opinions. It is important to reiterate that the focus group is a qualitative method of gathering information, concerned with understanding things rather than measuring them. Qualitative data can provide the library with important insight into user attitudes and needs; they cannot tell the library how many users feel the same way.

In their manual for libraries, Wagner and Mahmoodi provide a good summary of focus group objectives, which can serve as a reliable guide for libraries wishing to take advantage of this methodology. The authors believe that focus groups are an excellent way:

> *to obtain information from "those on the move" concerning the direction they are going; the needs they are experiencing; the changes they are observing; and the insights they have into the current situations; to identify trends, issues, and problems encountered, evolving or anticipated; and, to test suggested solutions and strategies, and to identify additional solutions and strategies [9].*

The methodology can be successfully employed by library staff in all types of settings as long as these basic objectives are understood and the focus group is not used in situations for which it was not intended. While there are many types of groups that are frequently made use of in the library: project teams, planning groups, standing committees, advisory boards, etc., the focus group is a special type of group, with its own special purpose. By understanding how the process works within this unique environment, library managers can avoid inappropriate use, while taking advantage of the many benefits of the focus group interview. The methodology can be a very useful one to add to their existing strategies for gathering information for planning and decision making.

REFERENCES

1. Krueger RA. Focus groups: a practical guide for applied research. 2nd ed. Thousand Oaks, CA: Sage Publications, 1994:34.
2. Valentine B. Undergraduate research behavior: using focus groups to generate theory. J Acad Libr 1993 Nov; 19(5):300–4.
3. Sevier R. Conducting focus group research. J Coll Admiss 1989 Win;122:4–9.
4. Gray-Vickrey P. Gerontological research: use and application of focus groups. J Gerontol Nurs 1993 May; 19(5):21–7.
5. Debus M. Methodological review: a handbook for excellence in focus group research. Washington, D.C.: Porter Novelli, 1988:2.
6. Morgan DL. Focus groups as qualitative research. Newbury Park, CA: Sage Publications, 1988:21.
7. Morgan DL, ed., Successful focus groups: advancing the state of the art. Newbury Park, CA: Sage Publications, 1993:11.
8. *Ibid.*, 1.
9. Wagner MM, Mahmoodi SH. A focus group interview manual. New York: American Library Association, Continuing Library Education Network and Exchange Round Table, 1994:2.

6

THE MODERATOR

⚜

In a focus group project, the moderator has by far the most important role of anyone involved. Since the data produced by this methodology are derived from communication between the participants, it is critical that the moderator has sufficient skills to stimulate and encourage all group members to take part in the discussion. Just as the questionnaire determines the amount and usefulness of the data gathered for a survey, to a very large extent the moderator determines both the quality and quantity of input which a focus group can generate. While good questions and careful preparation are essential, how the questions are asked, how focused the discussion remains, and to what extent the participants are willing to talk, are the keys to a successful focus group project. All these rely on the abilities of the moderator. Because of their central role, this chapter will review the knowledge and skills needed for a successful moderator, and some of the factors affecting those skills. Given these requirements, library managers will need to weigh the advantages and disadvantages of using a professional moderator over a librarian. This chapter presents some of the important factors to consider in making that decision and concludes with an overview of the moderator's role.

Moderator Skills and Characteristics: Although there are no licensing requirements for moderators of focus groups, nor any specific academic training, there is general agreement on the basic qualifications for this activity. Among the more important attributes are the ability to work with groups, to be a good listener, and to communicate clearly. The Advertising Research Foundation recommends that focus group moderators should be able to: quickly establish rapport with the group; encourage free expression among participants; think and act quickly; and listen attentively. Moreover, these individuals should be genuinely interested in respondents, alert to non-verbal responses, instinctive, intuitive, and objective [1]. Two other characteristics mentioned by Greenbaum as important to the moderator are being well-organized and having an excellent short-term memory [2]. This last point is important because the ability to remember a significant comment in the middle of a long response and return to it for further discussion, can often bring out important issues that might otherwise be lost. Finally, in describing what a moderator is not, Debus cautions that moderators are not teachers or judges; they never look down on respondents, and they do not agree or disagree with what is said. Neither do moderators put words into the mouth of a participant [3].

TABLE 6–1

MODERATOR CHARACTERISTICS

- People-oriented
- Good communicator
- Good interviewer
- Interested in topic
- Well-organized
- Good short-term memory

Looking at moderators from another perspective, a study by Tuckel et al., interviewed individuals who had recently attended focus groups. Asked to describe the characteristics of moderators that made them feel most comfortable; being friendly, down-to-earth, unthreatening, and having a sense of humor, were rated the most highly [4]. On the other hand, moderators were criticized if they were not able to ask good follow-up questions, or if they were not engaged energetically in the discussion. These observations highlight the importance of the moderator's ability to establish and maintain a genuine personalized, albeit brief relationship with members of the focus group. Because of the importance of this relationship, anything that influences or detracts from it can be critical. Issues such as age, sex, and race are potentially important here because cultural characteristics can seriously affect communication. For example, too large a gap in age between the moderator and group participants might lead to misunderstandings because of differences in word choice and usage. Different cultures have varying responses to age and sex, which could lead for example, to too much deference to an older moderator or conversely, a tendency to not take a younger moderator seriously. As a further example, a group of men might react differently to a male moderator than they would with a female leading the group. Even items such as mode of dress can unwittingly set up a barrier between moderator and participant.

McCracken, in discussing the moderator-participant relationship, describes the need for a blend of formality and informality in how the moderator approaches those in the group [5]. Factors such as the seriousness of the questions asked, and the professional attitude of the moderator can demonstrate to participants the importance of their contributions, as well as reassure them of the confidentiality of the process. A certain amount of informality, on the other hand, can help establish rapport and convince participants that the moderator is an understanding and sympathetic person. This, in turn, will contribute to the open atmosphere necessary for a successful discussion. Good moderators will quickly evaluate the personality of the group as well as specific individuals, and will adjust their own approach and tone accordingly. In general, the characteristics needed for moderating are those of an engaging and successful conversationalist; an individual who encourages others to speak out, pays attention to what they say, takes them seriously, and responds appropriately.

Professional vs. In-House: Because of the importance of this role, many organizations look for professional moderators when considering the use of focus groups. Indeed, moderating has become a highly successful business, and agencies exist in many cities that can supply a moderator for most types of projects. While selection of a moderator is usually not an issue in the academic research setting, where this position is usually filled by a member of the research team, in the business or organizational setting, there are various options to be considered. Opinions in the literature differ about the merits of using an outside professional rather than an individual within the organization. While some believe strongly that the person acting as moderator should have no personal stake in the project (see for example, Sevier [6]), others feel that insiders, with their in-depth knowledge and understanding of the general environment, are better able to lead discussions. Objectivity and background knowledge are seen to be at least partially in conflict.

Professional moderators clearly have several advantages. Because they come from the outside, they are not subject to the influences of the organization's employees and hence can be more objective in their approach and conduct of the focus group [7]. Neither do they have a stake in the outcome of the project, so that the results are not likely to be biased. Moreover, their training and experience ensure important skills in leading the group, coping with difficult situations, maintaining control of the discussion, and providing a careful analysis of the results. While these are all important factors, it is possible for a moderator to be too objective. If professional moderators are to be used in the library setting, careful consideration should be given not just to their experience in running other focus groups, but to how much they are interested in learning about the library's unique characteristics, and their willingness to work with the staff in preparing appropriate questions. A professional moderator must become sufficiently involved with the library to understand its situation, resources, and personnel in the light of the focus group topic.

There are, on the other hand, certain inevitable disadvantages in using an outsider, however skilled in conducting focus groups. An immediate problem, especially for non-profit organizations like libraries, is the cost. While charges vary, costs for a professional to conduct a focus group project (in 1997) are frequently quoted as between $3,000 and $5,000, money that smaller libraries are unlikely to be able to afford, even if contemplating major changes in programs or services. Although cost is often the first consideration, of equal concern is appropriate knowledge and understanding about the organization of a library, which most outsiders would lack. This can have serious effects on the quality and usefulness of the information resulting from the group discussions. For library projects, an outside moderator with little understanding of issues facing today's libraries might be less effective in directing the group discussion so as to draw out what is most relevant. Just as important, this lack of background can hamper even the most skilled moderator in knowing when to pull back from an unproductive topic or when to probe for more information [8]. Certainly a moderator with expertise in the topic is better able to hear the nuances in a discussion and can therefore learn more from the group than someone new to the library environment.

Selecting a Professional: It is therefore important if a professional moderator is used, that individual should be knowledgeable and sympathetic to the peculiar needs of the library, and, if possible, experienced in leading focus groups on behalf of library clients. In selecting potential consultants to work with, Krueger offers some good advice in determining their suitability. He recommends that prospective users ask questions about how much experience consultants have had conducting groups; whether or not they specialize in particular areas; how long they have been in business; and if they can provide a list of their past clients to contact for references [9]. For the library, it would also be important to know if they have worked with libraries or other non-profit, service organizations before, and then to contact these organizations to determine their level of satisfaction with the professional focus group organizer.

Finding any suitable consultant to work with can be difficult when this is a completely new experience to the librarian. The Web is one place to start, since some companies and individuals who conduct focus groups advertise their work through this medium. A few of them provide information on their areas of specialization and even provide a list of past clients. Almost none of them however, provide information on the costs of their services. Finding prospective companies or consultants, like finding any subject on the Web, depends on the search engine used, and the individual's patience in searching through multiple sites and screens. Looking in the yellow pages of a local phone book may also be useful. For example, in the Los Angeles telephone book, under the topic Marketing Research and Analysis, possible companies are listed. However, not all of these use the focus group technique and few provide more than a name and telephone number in the listings, so finding prospective consultants usually means calling each company individually. Word of mouth, or contact with a library director whose institution has described their focus group project in the literature, are other good ways of finding a consultant, and of course such individuals will have had experience in the library setting.

Apart from learning about their work with library focus groups, the initial interview with any prospective consultant is the time to determine exactly which services are included in their fee; how their charges are determined; and the amount of time estimated for the project. Charges can vary considerably in amount, as well as in the way they are determined. Some consultants charge an overall fee for a focus group project (*e.g.*, $3,500), while others break down fees into various categories:

- Recruitment
- Incentives for focus group participants
- Rental of facility
- Refreshments at the site
- Moderating
- Transcribing tapes
- Analysis and reporting
- Videotaping if required

Others charge a flat fee for on-site time at the library to conduct the groups (*e.g.*, $650 per day), while preparation and analysis time is charged on an hourly basis ($150 per hour). When working with this type of fee structure, it is very important to determine how many groups could be conducted in a day, and get a good estimate of the number of hours involved. Many consultants only provide the complete range of services for what they charge, including all the activities listed above; others may be more flexible and work with library staff so that they, rather than the consultant, assume some of the duties, such as contacting participants, arranging space, etc. This can result in at least some savings on the overall cost of the project. However much or little responsibility the library staff assume, it is extremely important that someone from the library, with a clear understanding of the library's goals, work closely with the consultant, especially at the start. This type of cooperation will help ensure that these goals remain the guiding principles of the entire project.

The overall decision to use a professional or a non-professional consultant can be a difficult one, and the library manager making this decision needs to weigh certain considerations. Perhaps the most important questions to ask are: why is the focus group project being utilized? who is requesting that the project be conducted? and how significant and/or costly are the likely outcomes? If the project is being conducted at the request of the institutional administration, rather than the library, results gathered by a professional consultant might be judged as more credible and less self-serving. This can also be true if the results will be used by the library to request a significant increase in the budget. Projects wholly under the control of the library, and those that are concerned with less potentially costly outcomes, are perhaps better candidates for in-house involvement. Whatever the decision, the overall investment of time and money, should be carefully weighed against the value of the potential results.

Non-Professional Moderators for the Library: Although marketing and business organizations primarily use the services of a professional moderator, lay moderators are being successfully used by service organizations and in the public sector where budget restraints may prohibit the utilization of expensive professionals. Libraries that are unable to hire a professional consultant do have various options for conducting focus groups, which can be inexpensive yet result in useful information. In the university setting, faculty members and graduate students trained in sociology or psychology can be a good and readily available alternative. These individuals have often developed useful skills in qualitative research techniques and will have experience in conducting interviews and working with people. Moreover, because they are themselves involved in research, they will have at least some understanding of libraries and their services. Likewise, individuals from marketing or communications programs on campus might be of assistance. While these individuals are literally on site for the academic library, many hospital libraries, depending on their location, can also take advantage of their services, potentially at little or no direct cost to the library budget.

In the library setting, however, the use of librarians as non-professional moderators should be seriously considered. Certainly these individuals, whether from in-house or from a similar institution, are likely to have both knowledge of and sympathy for the problems of a library. While few will have been trained in focus group interviewing techniques specifically, many librarians have developed some of the important skills needed by a moderator, which can be adapted successfully to this situation. Reference librarians, specifically, are usually accomplished at interviewing and have learned to probe for more information during the reference interview. Many have excellent interpersonal skills and know how to listen carefully and encourage people to articulate their information needs. They know how to keep a patron "on track," ask appropriate questions, and make their interaction both friendly and productive.

Given these abilities, interested librarians should be able to readily learn how to run successful focus groups. This book can provide an introduction to both the theory and practice of focus group interviewing as applied specifically to library situations. It should help a librarian both to identify questions that are answerable to focus group study and to organize and run a successful group interview. In addition to this work, there are several practical books and articles available that can provide further background knowledge and help identify additional skills needed to moderate a group. Particularly, there are a few basic texts, such as those by Greenbaum [10], and Krueger [11], which offer "how to" instructions and useful advice. While these works were not written specifically with library discussion topics in mind, the background information and many of the individual techniques discussed are useful in any focus group setting. The brief manual by Wagner and Mahmoodi [12], which was written specifically for librarians, although it was not intended to provide any in-depth assistance with running discussions or analyzing results, is helpful in describing the tasks involved in focus group projects, as well as by providing some good examples of library-related discussion questions. There are also innumerable examples in the journal literature of focus group applications. By reading some of these descriptions, librarians can gain a better understanding of where the focus group technique can be most successfully applied. Many of these articles also include useful sections on how to run a group, tips on moderating, as well as advice on such practical aspects as screening participants, or preparing the room.

Practicing with colleagues and co-workers can also be helpful for the novice moderator. By bringing together a mock focus group within the library, the various moderating techniques such as those described in chapter nine can be practiced until they become "natural" to the moderator. Including an observer in these groups, who can watch the moderator as well as the participants, can also be helpful. This individual can monitor moderator behavior: what techniques are used to encourage discussion? how clearly are questions asked? and how much probing is used? It is also useful to observe the group's reactions to the moderator. Providing this type of non-threatening setting and feedback can help aspiring moderators to sharpen their skills and become comfortable in their role.

Because there are no specific qualifications or licensing requirements for moderators, it is difficult to find programs or individual classes aimed specifically at developing focus group interviewing skills. Some classes do exist, taught at community colleges or by consultants who conduct focus groups as part of their businesses, but finding them may not be easy. Moreover, since the skills, knowledge, and experience involved in moderating and conducting focus groups are drawn from diverse disciplines, including sociology, psychology, and marketing, librarians would probably not have the time to pursue the variety of courses needed to give them a solid formal background. However, enrolling in classes that cover group leadership and facilitation, and provide a basic understanding of group dynamic, can provide useful background and techniques. The lack of specific training and educational opportunities aimed at the practicing librarian can perhaps be best remedied by their professional associations. Some steps have been made in this direction by two of the major library organizations. The American Library Association Continuing Library Education Network and Exchange Round Table was responsible for the first focus group manual aimed at librarians, which, though brief, provided some guidance in conducting groups [13]. Likewise, the Medical Library Association is responsible for publication of this volume. As a qualitative research methodology, focus group interviewing falls within the many skills needed by today's librarians to develop appropriate services to meet the ever changing needs of their users. Development of such skills fits into the missions of these associations [14]. Alternatively, courses on the focus group technique might also be included in library and information science graduate programs. Many schools already include general classes in research methodology; focus groups as an example of a qualitative research technique could logically fit into that portion of the curriculum.

Using In-House Staff: In contemplating the use of a librarian to lead a focus group, it is natural for libraries to first consider their own staff. There are definite advantages to this: who else can be as familiar with the library environment and the particular situation under investigation? Clearly in-house staff will have a good understanding of both the users and the services that may be scrutinized, and an important stake in the outcome of the project. No other moderator is likely to be nearly so knowledgeable or so involved in the questions under consideration.

There are, however, problems in using in-house staff. Apart from their overall lack of experience with the focus group technique, a big concern, because of their closeness to the topic being discussed, is that library staff will have a tendency to listen to what they want to hear. It is difficult to be objective when the topics are those which individuals are involved with on a daily basis. The danger in such a situation is that negative remarks might be ignored or suggestions that could result in significant changes for staff members might be dismissed. A staff member might, knowingly or not, direct the discussion away from an area that is personally or professionally threatening. In addition, participants may be reluctant to talk candidly when a library staff member is present. Many individuals might find it difficult in such a setting to make critical comments about the library services or staff, particularly if they know that in the future they may be approaching that person for help. A user, for example, might be reluctant to comment adversely about online search services, knowing that he or she will be needing a search for an upcoming project. As a result, with an in-house moderator, the discussion might have little real value for the library, because true opinions would not be voiced in an effort to avoid making negative or inflammatory statements. Just as difficult would be a session in which the opposite situation arose. Having a staff member available in a discussion group might be seen as an opportunity to complain about library services in general, especially if the staff member is in a position to set policies. Individuals might use the focus group as an excuse to talk about their personal problems with the library, including those that are totally unrelated to the topic of the discussion.

An alternative approach to using one's own staff is to recruit the services of a librarian at another institution. This individual may have a good understanding of the library's situation and concerns, yet find it easier to maintain objectivity because of a lack of personal involvement in the institution. This can be a useful alternative for hospital librarians since they are often situated in a one-person library. Another solution, for larger libraries, is to use a staff member from a department that is not directly connected with the subject under discussion. For topics concerning end-user training, for example, a librarian from the technical services department or interlibrary loans could serve as a knowledgeable moderator, yet one far enough removed from the training issues.

The Moderator's Role: Whether or not an in-house moderator is to be used, this decision should be made as early as possible in the process so that the individual can be involved in the preliminary steps needed before the actual discussions begin. The extent of this involvement will vary. In library situations where a small number of internal staff are used to conduct a focus group project, the moderator will most likely have several responsibilities. Apart from conducting the actual discussions, this individual may be involved in developing questions and in selecting participants, as well as in some of the more mundane aspects of the projects. If an outside consultant is used, the extent of this person's involvement will be determined during negotiations for services performed. In either case, close collaboration with the library manager is important to ensure that the project remains on target and meets the library's goals.

Whatever their role in the preparatory steps for focus group interviewing, clearly the moderator's major task is in leading the discussion and eliciting sufficient and appropriate information from all the group members. Debus describes the two major aspects of how a moderator approaches this task: through the questioning technique and through the way in which the entire group discussion is allowed to flow [15]. In terms of questioning technique, the moderator can use either a directive or non-directive approach. Non-directive questions are open-ended and include no bias or restrictions on the part of the moderator. The group members are free to answer in any way and take any direction they choose. For example, a typical non-directive question might be: What are your reactions to using the online catalog? In comparison, the directive approach would ask: What problems did you encounter when searching for subjects in the online catalog? This type of question is much more pointed and restricts the participants' range of response. It forces the group members not only to focus on subject searching but to think only about the negative aspects. It also gives much more control to the moderator. There may of course be times when a more specific question is needed. In general, non-directive questions are better able to elicit information on how library users feel about and react to library issues, by allowing the users to bring up what is important to them rather than what is important to the moderator.

The second major approach to focus group moderating is through the overall management of the group discussion. Here again there are two methods: structured and non-structured. In a structured group, the moderator will direct the discussion by using a pre-determined topic guide or specific set of questions which cover all the issues, including suitable prompts so as that nothing will be missed. For example, in a focus group discussing Internet use by physicians, a question about the barriers to access might include moderator prompts on cost, service providers, attitudes of hospital administration, and so on. In a non-structured group, however, such a discussion would start with a general question to get things started, then the group would take over. The participants rather than the moderator would determine what barriers to talk about. Most focus groups will use a structured, or at least a semi-structured approach, because leaving everything up to the group can mean many areas of the topic are not discussed. Morgan feels that this is quite appropriate when the researcher has a clear idea of the important questions to be asked and the type of information to be learned [16]. However, in the early stages of a project, unstructured groups can be very helpful in defining a problem and developing hypotheses. If, for example, use of a particular library service has declined significantly and the library does not know why, this type of focus group could perhaps bring out the reasons. Then, a more structured group could probe these areas for more information.

A non-directive, structured moderating approach can be the most useful in the library setting. A good moderator can keep enough structure and focus to ensure that the conversation remains on target, while providing sufficient freedom of response that participants will be able to tell the library what is really on their minds. Further details about conducting the focus group discussion and the types of questions and prompts that are needed are provided in later chapters. When the discussion is concluded, the moderator's final role is to analyze the results of the focus group and prepare a report. This might be a formal written report or an oral debriefing. Chapter ten covers the analysis and reporting phase of the project in more detail.

Clearly the moderator is a key player in conducting a successful focus group project. In the library setting, this individual can often be involved in much more than just the discussion. The library moderator is often responsible for all facets of the process from the initial development of the questions to preparing the final report. In considering the various duties of this individual, it is evident that librarians do have the potential for successfully fulfilling this important role. Good organization and communication skills; working well with people and in groups; asking open ended questions; listening carefully and probing for further information; all of these are important for a librarian, especially one who works with the public. By learning other, more specific techniques, practicing with colleagues, and observing groups in action, interested librarians should be able to adapt their existing skills to successfully use the focus group interview for assessing user needs and measuring the quality of their programs and services.

REFERENCES

1. Advertising Research Foundation. Focus groups: issues and approaches. New York: The Foundation, 1985:15.
2. Morgan DL, ed. Successful focus groups: advancing the state of the art. Newbury Park, CA: Sage Publications, 1993:76.
3. Debus M. Methodological review: a handbook for excellence in focus group research. Washington, D.C.: Porter Novelli, 1988:36.
4. Tuckel P, Leppo E, Kaplan B. A view from the other side of the mirror. Markt Res 1993 Fall; 5(4):24–7.
5. McCracken G. The long interview. Newbury Park, CA: Sage Publications, 1988:25.
6. Sevier R. Conducting focus group research. J Coll Admiss 1989 Win;122: 4–9.
7. McClelland SB. Training needs assessment data-gathering methods: Part 3, focus groups. J Eur Indust Train 1994;18(3):29–32.
8. Wells WD. Group interviewing. In: Ferber R., ed. Handbook of marketing research. New York: McGraw Hill, 1974:2–142.
9. Krueger RA. Focus groups: a practical guide for applied research. 2nd ed. Thousand Oaks, CA: Sage Publications, 1994:226.
10. Greenbaum TL. The handbook for focus group research. New York: Lexington Books, 1993.
11. Krueger, op. cit.
12. Wagner MM, Mahmoodi SH. A focus group interview manual. New York: American Library Association, Continuing Library Education Network and Exchange Round Table, 1994.

13. *Ibid.*
14. Medical Library Association. Platform for change. Chicago: The Association, 1991.
15. Debus, op. cit., 30.
16. Morgan DL. Designing focus group research. In: Stewart MA, Tudiver F, Bass MJ, Dunn EV, Norton PG, eds. Tools for primary care research. Research methods for primary care, v.2. Newbury Park, CA: Sage Publications, 1992:177–93.

7

PREPARING FOR THE DISCUSSION

~⁂~

Conducting a focus group project involves a series of steps that will be the topics of the next several chapters. In Table 7–1, these steps have been outlined in a series of phases, to provide a guide for library managers contemplating such an activity. While the phases proceed logically from beginning to end of the project, steps within phases can often be taken simultaneously or in a somewhat different order. However, by following this general approach, a project should proceed efficiently and effectively, and all the important steps will be covered. This chapter will look at the important, preliminary phases: determining project goals, selecting the project team, choosing participants, and selecting a suitable location.

Project Goals: Although it may seem self-evident, the first and most important step is to define just exactly why such a discussion should be conducted and what specifically it can achieve. A focus group without clear goals and a defined set of discussion topics is likely to degenerate into a vague and unproductive "gripe session." Because, as described in chapter one, there are other methods for collecting data and evaluating situations, it is important to determine whether or not the focus group technique will be the most effective method for each specific question, plan, or problem. To do this, a useful strategy is for the library manager to write out a description of the problem or situation facing the library, including all the background details that may help with clarification. After this is completed, the next step is to set out what the library sees as the end result of the project, that is, how the information gathered will be utilized and by whom, to resolve the situation.

As an example, because of changes in requirements for hospitals in managing information, as laid down by the Joint Commission on the Accreditation of Healthcare Organizations, a hospital library that had not served patients in the past may decide to extend service to both in-patients and out-patients. In such a situation, a logical first step might be to determine just what types of services the patients themselves might expect from the library, as well as the expectations of the health professionals who will be providing their care. It would also be important to clarify how much in the way of resources and staff time library management is able and willing to devote to patient services,

TABLE 7–1

PLANNING AND IMPLEMENTING A LIBRARY FOCUS GROUP PROJECT

PHASE I:

- Identify and discuss the problem/question to be researched
- Decide that focus groups are the appropriate method to collect data
- Identify those who will be involved in implementing the project and what roles each will play
- Decide on participant pool and criteria for selection

PHASE II:

- Begin to formulate questions
- Draw up a budget, time-line, and plan of action, including a list of tasks, and equipment and supplies needed
- Decide if and how participants will be remunerated
- Estimate number of sessions to be held
- Develop screening questions as needed for selecting participants
- Decide on site, dates, and times of sessions

PHASE III

- Work with appropriate groups, individuals to identify possible participants
- Screen potential participants and get commitments for more people than the minimum required
- Finalize questions

PHASE IV

- Call to remind participants 1–2 days before session
- Set up room with table, chairs, refreshments, recording equipment
- Run session(s) and record discussion
- Hold debriefing immediately after session(s)

PHASE V

- Have notes and tapes transcribed
- Review transcription, notes, and tapes as needed to analyze data
- Discuss findings among team members, check back with participants as needed for verification
- Write up findings and prepare report (oral or written) for library management
- Discuss findings with management
- Make decisions based on project findings and convey decisions to staff
- Thank participants and inform them of the results and decisions made

given its commitments to existing primary users. Questions can then be devised that will not generate unrealistic hopes or expectations in the focus group participants. Information on other local resources and the extent to which they are currently used by hospital clientele might also be very useful. By reviewing the whole situation, it should become clear what types of information are needed to initiate the new services, and who are the most likely groups of people to provide the necessary information. The library manager might then logically decide that focus group discussions with current patients and selected hospital staff might prove very useful in determining both patient needs and the expectations of both patients and staff for the new services. A more quantitative survey of resources in other local hospitals and public libraries would give additional necessary background information. Indeed, information from the focus groups might be useful in wording the survey sent to local libraries, since the discussions would probably reveal the types of information, *e.g.*, videotapes, specific language materials, which patients would most like to have available, and which staff believe would be most useful.

The Focus Group Team: Once the decision has been made to use focus group discussions, the next consideration is to decide who will actually conduct the project. While formal research projects that involve focus group interviews may be quite large and include an actual team of several professional researchers, the technique as used in the library setting is more likely to involve just a few individuals who may act in several overlapping capacities. The size and role of the team will depend primarily on whether or not an outside professional is hired to run the project, the scope of the project, and the size of the library staff. Some projects may involve an overall steering group responsible for initiating the work, determining the staff to be included, and reviewing and acting on the results, as well as an implementation team which makes all the arrangements, conducts the discussions, and analyzes the results. Whatever the ultimate number and configuration of players, however, it is important that the library manager maintain some level of involvement throughout, in order to provide validity for the project and the necessary authority for its implementation.

If an outside consultant or marketing company is used, the makeup of the team will depend on the individual company. However, it is important that the library maintain some level of involvement in the project. While the library director will need to meet initially with those brought in to run the focus groups, some other library staff member may be appointed as a continuing liaison. Whoever is involved from the library, close communication with the outside group will ensure that the library's goals are clearly understood and adhered to throughout the project. If library staff are conducting their own project, the number of staff involved will vary depending on the size of the library and the topic under consideration. Larger libraries may involve several members of staff, depending on the topic; for example, a project aimed at public services might include the head of reference and/or one of the reference librarians, as well as support staff to help make arrangements. In small libraries, the focus group project team may consist of as little as two or three individuals: the library manager, the person acting as moderator (if this is not the manager), and another staff member to assist the moderator. The individual assisting the moderator can have a number of roles: helping with preliminary planning and question development; acting as an observer during the discussions; helping with the analysis; and contributing to the write-up and reporting. The person in this role may even serve as an alternate moderator if several groups are to be convened. The level of participation will depend on individual interest and experience, as well as the size and complexity of the project.

Whatever the size and configuration of the team, the moderator is the most critical member because this individual is responsible for the quality of the data gathered during the actual discussion. Since it is typically the library manager, or head of a library department who initiates the project, a good working relationship between this individual and the moderator is essential. Close communication between the two, especially at the start of the project, will ensure that the moderator has a clear understanding of what information is being sought and how it will be used. It is equally important that the moderator understand the extent of his or her role, and how much library management wants to be involved. If the same individual is serving as both moderator and project coordinator, this person must assume overall responsibility for the project in all its phases. However, an ongoing involvement of library management will make it easier for the library to "assume ownership" of the project and increase the likelihood that the results will be used [1]. Some reversals of normal working relationships may thus occur; the moderator will be in charge of the focus group project, with the library director taking a secondary position. But once the project is completed, the library director will be responsible for any implementation, and the moderator may be completely removed from the picture. Both parties must be prepared to work within these changing relationships.

With the basic preliminaries taken care of, a general plan of action should be drawn up by the implementation team, with approval of the library manager. This should include: 1) a schedule or time line for the entire project; 2) a budget to cover expenses such as refreshments for focus group participants, taping costs, reimbursement for the moderator and/or participants if desired; and, 3) a clear delineation of the responsibilities of each team member. In many cases, the plan may not need to be elaborate, especially if only one or two discussion sessions are scheduled. However, a formal plan is especially helpful if an outside moderator is used, since then the expectations and obligations are unquestionably clarified. Moreover, if the library has never conducted this type of project before, such a plan can be useful in future discussions that may involve additional focus groups or other means of gathering information. If the project proves useful, a clear plan that defines expectations and obligations may become an integral part of the library's mechanism of ongoing assessment of needs.

Participant Selection: When the preliminary preparation is completed, the implementation team will begin to focus on the questions to ask and who will answer them. Because of its importance, consideration of how to construct useful questions is covered in a separate chapter. Once the questions have been determined in at least a preliminary form, the next important step in preparation for the project is selection of the participants. While the methods for selecting those to be included are much less strict than those used in quantitative research projects, care must be taken to choose both an appropriate and adequate group of individuals. Even though selection usually begins once the goals and topic have been clarified, it may not necessarily end here. With qualitative methods such as the focus group, the need for additional sessions may be determined once discussions actually start and data are reviewed.

Criteria for selection are determined by the topic: individuals chosen must have some knowledge of that topic because they have had either past or current experience with it. In most cases, therefore, the group of individuals to chose from will be self-evident. In a library setting, for example, a focus group project may be concerned with the adequacy of reading and study space in the library. In this case, it would be important to include at least some individuals who actually spend time on site. However, if electronic access to library resources is being considered, other criteria for participant selection would need to be used; at least a few of the participants should have made use of these techniques. If the focus group project is concerned with developing services for a particular group such as students, pharmacists, or nurses, obviously participants would be selected from those groups. On the other hand, if more general services are being considered, representatives from several user groups may be needed and different responses will be anticipated. Although the criteria may seem self-evident, it is useful to document them since the selection of additional groups may be deemed necessary further along in the project. There should also be a description of the criteria within the final report.

While the major criterion for group membership is knowledge and/or experience, in some cases selection is based on some shared characteristic of interest to the library, such as in a study of non-users. Other factors to consider in selecting participants are their willingness to share their experiences, and, to at least some degree, their ability to reflect on them within the group environment. Participants need not have the same views, or come from the same background; they need only share a common experience related to the topic [2]. The focus group team plays an important part in defining the necessary qualifications of focus group attendees to ensure that individuals will be included who have opinions that will provide meaningful input to the discussion. By working closely with the library manager, the team can translate these characteristics into the identification of an appropriate group of specific individuals from the user population.

How Many Groups to Use: After deciding on the appropriate population from which to recruit participants, an initial decision must be made on how many discussion sessions will be conducted, even if this number is increased later on in the project. The overall number of sessions will be determined both by need and by the amount of time, money, or other resources the library has to commit to the project. Repeating a discussion with different groups brings out further insights and helps to validate the information obtained, so it is important to have more than one session on a particular topic whenever possible. Krueger gives a helpful rule of thumb, suggesting that sessions should be repeated until little new information is forthcoming [3]. Clearly, meeting this criterion may compete with the availability of time and resources for focus group organization and use. While the first two focus groups generally produce a good deal of useful and unique information, by the third or fourth session, much of the discussion has already been heard before. Krueger therefore recommends planning four sessions but evaluating the results after the third, so that if new information is no longer being recorded, the fourth can be safely canceled.

Another consideration in determining the overall number of sessions is based on the data that emerge from the initial discussions. Although many focus group projects will start with a clear set of goals and well-designed questions, early groups may identify additional areas, which are unexpected but which the implementation team considers important to pursue. This is in fact one of the unique benefits of this type of data collection method. Results do not depend merely on the initial ideas or proposals of the researcher, but can be expanded and enriched by the participants themselves as they develop new ideas and raise additional questions. When this happens, additional sessions may be needed to further explore these new areas. Knowing that this may occur, it is helpful to plan for at least one additional group beyond the number initially determined.

A final consideration when deciding on the number of groups needed is the type of project being conducted [4]. If the aim of the project is to answer some very specific questions, the discussions can be fairly well structured and a large amount of data will be collected from each individual group. For projects that are more exploratory in nature, however, this will not be the case. In this type of project, the sessions are much less structured, and little control is exerted by the moderator. Because participants are more free to control the topics and order of conversation, any individual session may be much less "efficient" in terms of data gathering. Such an unstructured approach will therefore almost certainly require a larger number of sessions to produce sufficient data for subsequent comparison and analysis.

Whatever the final number of groups held, repetition to ensure a wide range of opinion and validation of the information gathered is important when the library is using the technique for important decision-making. If it is at all possible, any group of users that might influence the effectiveness of the changes or new services contemplated should be included [5]. This is especially critical when the library antic-ipates significant changes, and possibly a large commitment of resources to result from what is learned from the discussions. However, if the library has little time or funding to spare for the project, if partici-pants are carefully selected, a minimum of two groups, using a good moderator and carefully developed questions, can still provide useful information. Libraries need to balance the time and money necessary to run the focus groups, the importance of the results, and the likelihood that concrete actions will be taken.

Recruitment: Recruiting members has been described as the most time-consuming part of the whole focus group project. In Scharf and Ward's project at the University Library in Orlando, Florida, they calculated that they had to ask twenty individuals in order to get a single participant and even then only about one-half of those who volunteered actually showed up for the discussion [6]. This may have been an extreme case, but situations can arise in which potential participants will have little interest in the topic or commitment to the institution. It is therefore wise to plan for additional volunteers to compensate for those who will not appear when they promise to do so. It is also helpful to initially select individuals whom you consider to have a high level of interest, institutional commitment, and respon-sibility. One way to find willing participants is to recruit them from already established groups such as student organizations or specific departments within the institution. The leaders of those groups can be especially helpful in encouraging participation by members because their visible support can increase the legitimacy of the project.

Once suitable groups and individuals have been identified, partici-pation can be encouraged through some type of incentive. Business and commercial groups usually pay the individuals who attend their focus groups, as well as providing them with refreshments before the discussions begin. Library budgets may not extend to actual payments, but could include some type of "in kind" remuneration such as free photocopying or online printing privileges. And light refreshments provided at the start of the discussion can be an inexpensive but useful method of establishing a welcoming and relaxed atmosphere. Another way to encourage participation is to hold the focus group meetings during non-working hours, such as in the early evening, or on a weekend morning. Bringing individuals together when they are not in the middle of their daily work routine can promote the discussion, because their attention is less apt to be focused elsewhere, as well as make it more convenient for certain individuals to be included. However, while discussions held during non-working hours can be helpful for some participants, they may not work for others, such as parents with small children who must arrange for child care or individuals who live a long way from the site. Scheduling should try to take into account the convenience of the group in general, however there will never be a "perfect" time for a focus group discussion.

Facilitating transportation to the discussion site can be another incentive. In some focus group projects, for example, those that involve patients or elderly participants, providing transportation or covering the costs of parking, can be an important encouragement. This might be an important consideration for public libraries since their users can be drawn from a widespread geographic base. Such considerations are generally less important for the special library. In a hospital or academic health sciences library setting, projects that are concerned only with primary users may not need to take transportation concerns into consideration unless the discussions are held outside normal working hours. However, getting people to the discussion site can still be an issue, because even those arriving on foot can be discouraged if the site is a long way from their work place or in a room that is difficult to find.

The mix of individuals attending any single focus group is also important for its success. Most of the literature describing this methodology, whether in marketing studies or formal research projects, emphasizes the importance of homogeneity within the group [7]. Since the focus group is a social occurrence, the background, culture, knowledge level, and social position of the participants can be crucial in how the group interacts and thus affect the outcome of the discussion. Too broad a mix of individuals can be a problem, because their lack of commonality will make it much more difficult for them to form into a cohesive group, an essential element for the success of the focus group. In an academic library setting for example, mixing students with faculty could possibly lead to problems if the students are intimidated by the presence of their teachers. Students might be inclined to either keep quiet in deference to their lesser position in the academic environment, or not want to disagree with faculty members' opinions when these individuals potentially control student grades and recommendations. Alternatively, faculty might hesitate to show ignorance about a topic in front of their students. In the same way, when group members are recruited from a particular department in the parent institution, mixing staff and management could be a problem and lead to unequal participation if managers have sufficient influence over those who work for them, or, conversely, feel unprepared to deal with specific or technical aspects of work related to the focus group topic.

Another potential problem that may arise when recruiting people who know each other, either because they work closely together or are friends outside of the workplace, is that they can digress into personal conversations or problems and not keep focused on the discussion topic. While investigators differ in their responses to the use of acquaintances in focus groups, the little research that has been conducted in this area shows that the effects are minimal [8–9]. Nevertheless, when people who know one another well are engaged in discussion, they may not want to appear to disagree with each other for the sake of their friendship, or feel they cannot be totally candid, for example, with people they see every day at work. This lack of disagreement might lead the moderator to discern an unreal sense of homogeneity of opinion [10]. Using people who know one another can also encourage side conversations during the discussion, and it runs the risk of introducing established relationships into the group. If one participant is already recognized as a "leader," others might be hesitant to disagree with this person's opinions. On the other hand, personal relationships cannot be an automatic reason for excluding participants. Acquaintanceship can help the focus group, because it allows for more ease and naturalness in the discussion and assists the group in quickly creating an atmosphere conducive to conversation. In practice, it may not even be possible to avoid acquaintanceship in library focus groups, especially when the needs of a particular group of users, for example, members of a hospital department, are being investigated. A competent moderator should be able to keep the group on target, and overcome any tendencies to defer to "leaders," and encourage full participation by all members. This is most likely to occur when the moderator has made it clear that all responses are welcome, reasonable, and "correct."

Given these various requirements for focus group participants, it can be difficult, especially for a library in a small institution, to find enough suitable individuals. With an insufficient number of individuals to draw from, there is a genuine concern about both the typicality of those who attend, and their overuse. Individuals who participate in multiple focus group discussions can quickly become "experts." Even the best screening procedures cannot always eliminate these repeat participants. This familiarity with the focus group method can cause problems. Even with a new topic to discuss, the experiences from other discussions can affect the spontaneity of their response. This prior knowledge of group procedure can also encourage individuals to challenge the moderator, or in some other way dominate the rest of the group. Any of these reactions can have an adverse effect on the group, both in terms of group process and the quality of the discussion. The result is a less than optimal result for the organizer of the group. When selecting participants, it is therefore important to determine how much experience they may have had with the methodology and if possible, avoid individuals who have attended previous focus groups. If this is impossible, eliminating those who have attended recently can enhance the spontaneity and freshness of the group discussion.

Even in a large institution with a potentially wide supply of fresh participants, studies that are aimed at particular population groups— for example, one which is concerned with information access for residents in a hospital setting—can soon run out of suitable participants who are willing and able to give up their time to attend a session. These situations can result in the overuse of a few good participants or the inclusion of individuals who do not meet all the criteria for the project. Because of such limitations, some marketing companies that run focus groups have turned to virtual groupings, using telephone or videotele-conferencing to broaden their pool of attendees. This might be a consideration for academic medical centers whose users are located at outlying hospitals, clinics or laboratories. Certainly library organizations with a widespread membership might consider using such approaches with focus group discussions.

Contacting Participants: Once potential focus group members have been identified, they should be contacted by the moderator or another member of the project team. This is particularly important if other individuals, such as chairs of departments or leaders of existing groups, have been used to solicit focus group members. A personal contact with those who have agreed to participate, either by telephone, e-mail message, or letter, or by attending departmental or group meetings, will help to persuade participants that they are truly important to the project. This follow-up contact is also a good opportunity to help volunteers understand their roles in the focus group, and to encourage them to make a firm commitment to the process. The moderator is perhaps the individual most capable of achieving this. While a brief explanation of the project can help encourage participation, it is not a good idea at this time to go into detail about the kinds of questions to be asked. Some individuals might then feel the need to prepare for the discussion, by doing background research or discussing the issues with other people. While this type of preparation will clearly interfere with spontaneous discussion at the focus group, it can also encourage participants into thinking that they must suggest solutions, when the purpose is really to identify issues and problems.

A final issue that is of particular concern in the marketing and business use of focus groups is screening of participants for suitability. Business organizations take care to screen out unsuitable or undesirable individuals, such as a competitor's employees or members of the news media [11]. While a library normally does not share such concerns, it is a good idea to do some initial screening, to make sure that the most appropriate individuals are invited. A few basic questions can determine their level of knowledge and interest in the topic. For a focus group to review particular library services, it would be appropriate to find out if candidates had used that service, as well as to learn in general how much or little they use the library. The screening interview can also provide some idea of how forthcoming an individual is in conversation, and how opinionated. The manner in which a person answers these preliminary questions and how readily he or she is able to articulate responses can provide clues for future potential in the group. While the interview need not take very much time, it is worth the effort, especially if the topic for discussion is very specific. For example, if the library wants to learn about how individuals use a particular online tool, a few simple questions can determine if potential group participants have in fact used the tool and to what extent. For any focus group project, it is important to remember that the quality of the data produced generally reflects the quality of the participants [12].

Site Selection: A final step in preparing for the focus group discussion, and one that also has a bearing on how productive the discussion might be, is the selection and set up of a suitable room. Because location can effect the quality of the responses, the neutrality of the room is an important consideration. With the library as the subject of the discussion, a room outside the library is preferred. In this way, participants will feel more free to speak openly and, if necessary, critically about library issues. If the group must meet in the library, a comfortable room away from service areas could be appropriate. Since free discussion and interaction among group members is critical, the atmosphere of the room, wherever it is located, must be relaxed and inviting so that people are comfortable and encouraged to talk. Temperature is one factor in creating this atmosphere, where an overly warm room or one that is too cold, can be both uncomfortable and distracting. With the typical focus group lasting up to two hours, comfortable chairs are also very important. If possible they should be softer than those usually available for library study. Equally important is the arrangement of the chairs. In order to encourage discussion back-and-forth, they should be arranged so that participants face each other and are able to make eye contact with one another and with the moderator. Moreover, chairs should be set up so that participants are all roughly equidistant from the moderator. Chairs should never be set up in rows as in a classroom, because this arrangement minimizes interaction between participants and is associated with right and wrong answers [13]. Having a table around which the group is evenly spaced is the most useful arrangement; it emphasizes participant equality and allows members to lean forward without being conscious of their bodies, which might also hinder full participation [14]. To further encourage concentration on the discussion topic, outside distractions should be kept at a minimum. Rooms that are noisy or have windows looking out into busy areas, should therefore be avoided. A final consideration is how easily participants can find the room. Complicated directions is just one more reason for people not to show up.

Other than the table and chairs, the only other physical feature needed in the room is an electric outlet for plugging in the tape recorder. Even if the library is able to have a second staff member present to record the discussion, a tape recorder is extremely useful in capturing the entire conversation. Human recorders can be distracted and miss important comments. Moreover, being able to rely on the machine allows the individual to notice more than just the words being used. Sometimes body language can contribute important clues to how people feel and add other dimensions to the discussion. Since these cannot be captured on audiotape, the human recorder can make a note of any non-verbal clues, which might be useful while the machine continues to record the dialog. In some libraries, a videotape camera might also be used to capture this non-verbal input. Marketing groups that specialize in focus groups routinely use videotaping in recording discussions, often behind one-way mirrors or windows so that the camera is not intrusive. Although many libraries would not readily have access to this equipment or type of room set up, home video cameras can be successfully used, and with appropriate preparation of the participants, even an in-room camera can quickly recede into the background.

While these various preliminary steps may take considerable time, they are well worth the effort. Having a clear understanding of the purpose of the focus group project will not only facilitate the development of suitable questions, it will assist in defining the characteristics needed in the participants. Care in selecting a capable moderator and assembling a suitable team to carry out the project will avoid problems as the project advances. Even details such as setting up the interview room can contribute to the success or failure of the process. In the library setting as in any other, the quality of the preparation for focus group interviewing is an important factor in producing believable data in which library management can have full confidence.

REFERENCES

1. Aubel J. Guidelines for studies using the group interview technique. Geneva: United Nations, International Labour Office, 1994:13.
2. Holloway I, Wheeler S. Qualitative research for nurses. Oxford: Blackwell Scientific, 1996:146.
3. Krueger RA. Focus groups: a practical guide for applied research. 2nd ed. Thousand Oaks, CA: Sage, 1994:88.
4. Morgan DL. Designing focus group research. In: Stewart MA, Tudiver F, Bass MJ, Dunn EV, Norton PG, eds. Tools for primary care research. Research methods for primary care, v.2. Newbury Park, CA: Sage Publications, 1992:177–93.
5. Hambrick RS, McMillan JH. Using focus groups in the public sector: a tool for academics and practitioners. J Man Sci & Policy Anal, 1989 Sum;6(4):45–53.
6. Scharf MK, Ward J. A library research application of focus group interviews. In: The Association of College and Research Libraries' National Conference. Energies for transition. Chicago: The Association, 1986:191–3.
7. Merton RK, Fiske M, Kendall PL. The focused interview: a manual of problems and procedures. 2nd ed. New York: Macmillan, 1990:137.
8. Nelson JE, Frontczak NT. How acquaintanceship and analyst can influence focus group results. J Advertising 1988;17(1):41–8.

9. Fern EF. The use of focus groups for idea generation: the effects of group size, acquaintanceship and moderation on response quantity and quality. J Markt Res 1982;19(1):1–13.
10. Wells WD. Group interviewing. In: Ferber R., ed. Handbook of marketing research. New York: McGraw Hill, 1974:2–137.
11. Nasser DL. How to run a focus group. Publ Rel J 1988 March; 44(3):33–4.
12. Sevier R. Conducting focus group research. J Coll Admiss 1989 Win;122: 4–9.
13. Merton, Fiske, Kendall, op. cit., 139.
14. Krueger, op. cit., 48.

8

QUESTION DEVELOPMENT

⚶

Many people view the construction of questions as the hardest task involved in conducting qualitative research with the focus group methodology. After all, if you don't ask the right questions you won't get the information you want. This chapter will discuss some of the issues involved in developing appropriate questions. The structure of the questions; the actual words used; how many are asked, and in what order; as well as the use of follow-up prompts, will be addressed here because they are all important considerations in a successful focus group project. Some examples of both effective and non-effective ways of asking questions are included here; more examples can be found in the case studies described in the final chapter.

> ### TABLE 8–1
>
> #### FOCUS GROUP QUESTIONS MUST BE. . .
> - Clear and concrete in terminology and phrasing
> - Open-ended to encourage maximum participation
> - Free of library jargon
> - Precise and not overly long
> - Asked in a logical order from general to specific
> - Limited to 5–10 per session

There are two schools of thought on how far question preparation should be taken. Some researchers, who have used focus groups in formal and informal projects, advocate using a general topic outline, rather than specific questions [1]. Such an outline includes all the major issues for discussion, including how they relate to one another, and serves as a guideline for the moderator. This method, according to its proponents, provides greater flexibility for the moderator in dealing with individual groups. Since every discussion group is unique, a guide such as this, which allows the moderator discretion in bringing up topics and framing questions to best suit the situation, can be very effective. On the other hand there are those who believe in the importance of preparing specific questions for the group ahead of time, in order to allow the moderator to concentrate on leading the group and not having to formulate questions [2]. While this is particularly important for the sake of continuity if a large number of groups are to be convened and asked the same series of questions, it also serves to reduce moderator bias and lessens the stress and the need to react quickly and appropriately that may be difficult for a novice moderator. For library staff planning their first focus group project, particularly if the moderator will be a librarian with little experience in using the technique, it will almost certainly be more helpful to settle on precise questions that cover all the major issues. As long as they are worded so as to bring out the maximum amount of discussion and cover all critical topics, the moderator will find it easy, as he or she becomes more comfortable in this role, to rephrase or introduce questions in various ways appropriate to each individual group.

Once the decision has been made to use specific questions rather than a more general guide, the individuals responsible for their preparation, usually the implementation team, must be guided by the fundamental goals of the project to ensure that the questions asked will successfully gather the data needed to meet those goals. Although constructing good questions may appear daunting, most questions will develop naturally from a consideration of the topic under review. Indeed, the initial discussion between the implementation team and the library manager in reviewing the need for a focus group project may actually be cast in a series of questions, many of which can then be modified and used in the actual group interviews. For example, in a hospital library, the librarians may be concerned with an apparent under utilization of library resources by the nursing staff. They may decide to investigate the reasons for this through a series of focus group discussions that could help them gain a better understanding of nurses' information needs and practices. Through various interactions with nursing staff, library personnel may already have some ideas as why this group makes so little use of the library. Preliminary discussions about the focus group project may include speculations about lack of time, inadequate nursing resources, hours of service, etc., as possible contributing factors. These concerns would then be developed into a series of questions to be asked during the group discussions, including some prompts to make sure that all possible reasons are discussed. The hospital case study in chapter eleven provides more detail on the specific questions that might be used to deal with such nursing staff concerns.

Maximizing Discussion: In a project such as this, although library staff may be interested in gathering answers to specific concerns (are library hours too short? are there sufficient nursing textbooks?) asking questions in this limited way may fail to bring out other valuable information. Focus group questions should be constructed to encourage both the maximum amount of discussion and the free expression of what the participants think. Table 8–2 provides examples of "good" and "bad" ways to ask questions in a library focus group discussion. Questions that require limited, "yes" or "no" answers are clearly not productive in this environment. Referred to as dichotomous questions, they may seem an easy way to get a response but they do not evoke the breadth or depth of discussion or the clarity of response that the focus group is designed to obtain [3]. Neither are direct or closed-ended questions usually helpful since they can often produce a more anticipated rather than a spontaneous response. This type of question, in effect, forces the group participants to respond to specific issues or aspects of a topic, which may not really be what they have on their minds. The open-ended question because of its lack of structure, does not fix attention so specifically and creates what Merton et al. called a "blank page to be filled in by the interviewee" [4]. Clearly there must be some structure to the overall interview, or the group could talk about anything that comes to mind. It can be a difficult balance at times to provide enough direction in the questions to keep participants focused on the topic, yet enough freedom to say what they really think. Good planning is essential, as is the ability of the moderator to respond to specific comments and situations.

Prompts: One way to counter the effect of too little structure is through the use of prompts. For example, in the nursing example discussed earlier, a general question such as "What are the major barriers which prevent you from using the library?" is very open, as stated, and allows participants to spontaneously talk about the problems they encounter. After the initial responses have been given to such a question, however, there may be particular items that have not been mentioned but that the library feels are important. If this happens, the moderator can follow up the question by using prompts to stimulate discussion about these other items. These prompts are legitimate ways of broadening thediscussion; they are especially helpful in the early part of the interview when participants are most likely to be hesitant in responding. Yet there

TABLE 8–2
EFFECTIVE QUESTIONING IN FOCUS GROUP DISCUSSIONS

Ineffective Questions	Effective Questions
Do you go to the library when you need information?	*When you have an information question during the work day, where do you go for an answer?*
Encourages a yes or no answer.	Allows respondents to describe various sources used and can reveal the place of the library in their information-seeking.
What do you feel are the least important services the library offers?	*Imagine you are coming into the library for the first time: what are the things you would look for or ask about first?*
Difficult for people to assess what is least important to them; better to focus on what is most important.	Draws on actual experience of participants and reveals what is most important to them in terms of library services/resources.
Is the online catalog easy to use?	*What features of the online catalog do you find easiest/hardest to use?*
Encourages a yes or no answer; difficult to answer negatively without admitting ignorance or lack of skills.	Allows users to bring up personal experiences both good and bad in a non-threatening way.
How often do you request ILLs? How easy is it to submit your requests? Do you usually get ILLs in a timely manner?	*Can you describe your experiences with requesting journals or books which the library does not own?*
Encourages a yes or no answer to each question without the reasons behind the answers; uses library jargon.	Uses readily understood terminology; allows users to draw on their own experiences, both good and bad.

are drawbacks in using prompts, for with them, the moderator is in effect planting ideas in the minds of the participants rather than waiting for spontaneous disclosure. While the information given in response to the original, non-structured question demonstrates what the *participants* find as the biggest problems in using the library, the responses to the prompts reflect opinions on what the *library staff* believe to be the barriers. Thus, while prompts can be helpful, they should be used with care and weighed against the type of information that the question is designed to elicit. If they are used, it is better to wait until discussion comes to a natural conclusion, so that people have sufficient opportunity to reveal what is truly on their minds.

Open-ended, non-directive questions, those which provide group members with a wide choice of responses, are obviously the best type to use in the focus group interview. If, for example, library staff wants to learn about patron difficulties in using an online product so that effective training classes can be developed, asking participants "Have you used (the product)?" leaves little room for more than a simple yes or no response. If on the other hand the moderator asks: "Tell me about your experiences with (the product)," the door is opened for any type and level of response. Although it is the patrons' problems with the online product that are of specific interest, asking a question such as "Do you have problems using the online product?" would probably not bring out as much useful information. Not only could such a question be answered simply by yes or no, most people would probably say no. In such a situation, it is a natural reaction for people to not want to admit they cannot do something, especially if they think most or all of the other participants in the group can do it. Moreover, focusing on the word "problems" will ignore the positive experiences some participants might have had. Such experiences could in fact provide valuable insight in how people successfully approach an online product, information that could be useful for future training. If, on the other hand, the moderator asks participants "Can you describe your experiences with the online product?," participants will find it easier to talk about the problems they have encountered since they are also able to describe their successes.

Phrasing and Terminology: How the questions are asked is just as critical as what is asked. In conducting the focus group interview, the moderator must pose the questions that have been drawn up in clear and concrete terms, which are easily understandable by the group. Asking questions that are vague or too theoretical may limit the ability of the group members to respond or result in the production of vague or poorly considered responses that are of little real value. Likewise, using phrases that are too generalized, or questions that are too broad (What do you think of our library?), can result in answers which are correspondingly too general and which will reflect more socially acceptable opinions rather than those personally held by the participants [5]. Yet another problem is asking questions that are overly long and complicated. This can be confusing to people if they feel they must answer all parts of such a question; it can also be intimidating, turning the interview into more of an interrogation than a friendly discussion. Such an atmosphere is obviously not conducive to the open, honest discussion upon which a successful focus group is based.

As well as the importance of phrasing in focus group questions, the specific wording or nomenclature used is also of concern because unclear terminology can be misunderstood and lead to discussions that have no real bearing on the topic. Librarians need to be especially watchful of using too much jargon since patrons may be unfamiliar with many terms which library staff use all the time. Asking patrons to discuss their experiences with interlibrary lending, or even worse, with "ILL," may not be as effective as referring to this service from the patron's point of view, *i.e.,* getting materials for them which the library does not own. Apart from technical jargon, it is also important to keep the questions as neutral as possible because the use of some "hot" terms can bring strong reactions and turn the interview into a gripe session rather than a constructive discussion. Issues such as billing and overdue items can provoke such reactions, especially if participants have had recent experiences and feel frustrated. If these issues are to be discussed, the terms in which they are introduced can be crucial. Using more directed questions for these types of topics may help to keep the discussion open and informative. Asking: "How do you feel about receiving bills for overdue items?" may be too much of a trigger; a specific question posed in a more impersonal tone, such as: "How could the library best handle billing individuals for overdue items?" encourages a more general discussion. Overall it is more helpful to formulate questions in positive terms, as noted above, rather than in a negative manner whether or not the topic is a potentially explosive one [6]. That is not to say that questions about negative experiences should not be asked; it will simply be more profitable to encourage positive expression of frustrations and anger than to incite feelings that can hamper the success of the overall discussion. It is doubtful that you can learn much by making your focus group participants angry, embarrassed, or resentful.

Order and Number of Questions: In general, however directed or free flowing the structure of the discussion is, starting the session with a question that everyone can easily respond to (*e.g.*, What is the single most important thing you use this library for?) is a good way to warm up the group. By asking an "easy" question, which does not demand serious reflection, even the most timid participant can be reassured that the session will not be too threatening. This technique, especially when preceded by going round the room for general introductions, helps to develop a relaxed and open atmosphere early in the session, in which everyone feels comfortable giving their opinion.

Whatever type of question is used to begin the discussion, the general sequence for focus group questioning is to move from the general to the specific. Apart from lending a more natural flow to the conversation, it helps to develop a good framework of understanding for the moderator about the group's knowledge of the subject. Such a framework is useful in understanding and interpreting later comments on more specific aspects of the subject. Most importantly, asking general questions allows the key issues, as seen by the participants, to emerge naturally and spontaneously without direct influence by the moderator [7]. In a related approach, Wagner and Mahmoodi suggest an overall schedule for questioning that begins by asking participants to reflect on the present situation, moves on to having them project that situation into the future, and then asks participants to evaluate possible strategies for addressing the desired outcome in the future [8]. This too has the advantage of asking the easier questions first, because most people will find it simpler to describe their current experiences than to speculate about future possibilities. It also provides a logical structure for the discussion so that the ideas and opinions brought out at the beginning can help participants as they respond to the later, more challenging questions toward the end.

Apart from the order of the questions, another important consideration is how many questions should be asked during the session. A common danger is to try to ask too many. Ten questions is the maximum that most moderators use in a discussion, although half this number is not unusual. Given that most groups will meet no more than one to two hours, trying to cover more will only produce superficial results since there will not be time to cover any single topic in depth [9]. Two hours may seem a very long time to answer five or six questions, and an individual might easily accomplish that with time to spare. In a group situation however, those same questions will take up much more time since the answers from one person will provoke responses from another or remind a third of some related experience or idea. This is in fact the very heart of the focus group methodology and why it is so successful in exploring ideas. Individuals speak, listen, respond to others, modify their original comments, and elicit responses and adaptation of opinions from others in the group.

Finally, whatever the ultimate number and arrangement of the questions, it is important for the moderator to make sure that all of them are covered during the time allotted for the discussion. Pacing of questions is therefore important, so that not too much time is spent either on early topics or ones that prove to be particularly interesting to the group, to the detriment of other questions. This is not always easy to accomplish because no one wants to cut short a promising discussion. Knowing how to pace the questions and where discussion can be safely curtailed calls for a thorough understanding of the project's goals. Such knowledge will help the moderator determine the relative importance of each question and know where and when to speed up the group [10].

While there are many factors to consider in developing successful questions for a focus group project, clearly the most important one is to ensure that they are framed to gather the information needed to answer the questions or concerns of the project. By focusing on the project's goals the questions should come naturally. By taking time to word them clearly and unambiguously, in an open-ended structure, they should allow for the maximum amount of freedom for respondents to answer with their own ideas and opinions. For library staff new to this technique, it might be useful to test the questions first. Trying them out on colleagues can give a good indication as to the amount and type of response they generate. Better still is to test them with one or two individuals outside the library environment, to ensure that they are understandable and effective with the type of audience who might be expected to attend a focus group in the library.

REFERENCES

1. Advertising Research Foundation. Focus groups: issues and approaches. New York: The Foundation, 1985:12.
2. Paley N. Getting in focus. Sales & Mark Man 1995 Mar; 147(3 part 1):92–5.
3. Krueger RA. Focus groups: a practical guide for applied research. 2nd ed. Thousand Oaks, CA: Sage, 1994:58.
4. Merton RK, Fiske M, Kendall PL. The focused interview: a manual of problems and procedures. 2d ed. New York: Macmillan, 1990:15.
5. Krueger RA. Quality control in focus groups. In: Morgan DL, ed. Successful focus groups: advancing the state of the art. Newbury Park, CA: Sage Publications, 1993:77.
6. Aubel J. Guidelines for studies using the group interview technique. Geneva: United Nations, International Labour Office, 1994:26.
7. Debus M. Methodological review: a handbook for excellence in focus group research. Washington, DC: Porter Novelli, 1988:24.
8. Wagner MM, Mahmoodi SH. A focus group interview manual. New York: American Library Association, Continuing Library Education Network and Exchange Round Table, 1994:2.
9. Aubel, op. cit., 12.
10. Wells WD. Group interviewing. In: Ferber R., ed. Handbook of marketing research. New York: McGraw Hill, 1974:2–141.

9

CONDUCTING THE DISCUSSION

‹⁂›

While moderators can play an important part in the preparatory stages of focus group interviewing: developing the questions, selecting participants, coordinating participation, and arranging a meeting room; their major task is in leading the discussion. Whatever the topic under investigation, this phase of the project requires all of the moderator's skills to lead participants through a series of well-defined steps in which:

- The stage is set;
- Group members begin to speak out;
- The discussion develops and is focused on the key questions; and
- Closure is reached when all the questions have been answered.

Because the success of any focus group depends on effective group interaction, developing and maintaining a suitable environment is the moderator's primary task during each stage of the procedure. A relaxed, non-threatening climate is essential if the group is to function properly and the information group members provide is to be truly valid and useful. It is therefore important for the moderator to quickly establish rapport with group members, to explain clearly why they have been invited there, and promote their interest in the project to encourage active participation. Then, as the discussion ensues, the moderator must listen carefully to the responses, make sure that all members of the group participate and that they stay focused on the topic. Finally, the moderator must bring closure to the discussion by asking some type of final question to see if anything has been missed, or by allowing time for reflection or summing up by the group. Each of these stages of the discussion will therefore require different actions and draw on different abilities of the moderator.

Setting the Scene: In many ways, the first few minutes of a focus group can be the most critical. It is here that the moderator explains the purpose of the discussion, describes what will be happening over the next one or two hours, and defines the rules of the game. Knowing the purpose and procedure for the discussion, and especially what is expected of them, addresses any concerns that participants might have and allows them to relax and concentrate on the topic without fear of surprises or embarrassment. In most cases, the participants of the group will not be well acquainted, and they need to recognize and accept their common and supportive purpose in being there. If they are already acquainted, (*e.g.*, as co-workers) they may need to be reminded that during the group discussion their relationships with one another are changed. This is why in the opening stage the moderator should also convey to the group the importance of each of their contributions. If the participants are convinced that their individual input will be taken seriously and be useful in improving library services, they are likely to be enthusiastic about their roles. Finally, a tone should be set that shows the participants that they can and should enjoy themselves and be free to ask for clarification if they don't understand a question; that this is to be an interesting discussion and not a test, a debate, or a lecture.

This initial step can be accomplished by first having the moderator introduce himself or herself and then briefly explain why the group has been assembled. This is especially important if the moderator has not personally invited each member of the group. Providing a clear description of the project and what the library is hoping to achieve will help ensure that everyone starts the event with the same goal in mind. It is also useful to explain what the library will do with the information gathered from the discussion. This not only emphasizes the importance the library places on the group's feedback but also helps to make clear that suggestions made by the group will be used in the overall planning process and will not necessarily be implemented. The moderator's remarks can be as brief as in the following example:

> Thank you for taking the time to come to this discussion. We have asked you here today because the library is exploring the possibility of providing access to electronic journals for its users. These are a relatively new and quite different resource for the library to handle and we know that you have had some experience with them. We are going to be asking you some questions about those experiences and the information we learn from you will be used to help decide what types of journals if any, the library should subscribe to, and how they might best be made available to users. We'll start with what types of things you have encountered in using electronic journals, and what you like and don't like about them. Then we'll ask about how your use of these journals might be changing in the

future, and what impact that might have in your practice, research, or study. Finally we'll discuss some possible strategies the library might use to help you access these journals and integrate them with other library resources.

Providing this amount of detail takes only a few minutes yet it is extremely important to help the group start to focus their thoughts on the topic.

Once the scope and intent have been explained, the moderator should next remind people how long the discussion will take and then briefly explain the ground rules. These should stress the importance of everyone contributing and saying what is really on their mind. The moderator should also remind the group that there are no right or wrong answers; that the library is interested in their individual ideas and experiences. This is also the time to ask people to remember to speak one at a time, and loudly enough so that everyone can hear. Although this may have to be repeated later, it helps discourage people from beginning side conversations, which can be distracting to the rest of the group, and it is especially important when the proceedings are being taped. In all of this, it is important that the moderator should maintain a friendly, relaxed but businesslike tone that sets an atmosphere that is serious without being threatening.

If a tape recorder is being used during the discussion, participants should be informed that this is being done only to ensure that all comments are captured and not to single out individuals in any way. Krueger warns of too much attention to the tape recorder since it could inhibit conversation [1]. However, if the conversation is recorded, it should never be done in secret; that would be an unethical invasion of privacy. It is also important to help the group understand that the information they provide will be treated as "group data" and that no particular answer will be attributed to an individual [2]. The moderator should also use this opportunity to encourage people to be open and frank in their remarks, and to stress that people will not necessarily agree with one another. In fact, the more views the library hears from the group, the better since only a small number of people can be reached with the focus group technique [3]. It may also be helpful to state that negative as well as positive comments are welcome. Negative remarks can sometimes be the most useful [4]. For instance, in the example given above dissatisfaction with the electronic journals format or a frank unwillingness to use it would be very important to know about and to explore. However, care should be taken not to overemphasize the role of negative comments to avoid the impression that the session is designed for participants to vent their grievances.

By taking the time to delineate the whys and hows of the focus group discussion, the moderator sends a message to the participants that their contributions are valuable and that the library is sensitive to their point of view and really cares about their perspective. This is also the opportunity for the moderator to project his or her own enthusiasm for the topic, which is critical in setting the tone for the ensuing discussion. Indeed, this whole preliminary part of the focus group can be a key to its success or failure. Projecting the right mix of interest, openness, and respect for people's opinions is the major role for the moderator before the actual discussion begins. Moreover, this preliminary sharing of information helps in the bonding between group members and the moderator, which is essential for good group interaction. It is also important at this point that the group "buy in" to the project, right from the start, because that can help ensure an energetic and open discussion. On the other hand, the moderator should not spend too much time on the introduction, since stressing issues such as the importance of negative comments might bias the ensuing discussion.

Group Members Speak Out: After the preliminaries have been completed, it is time for the members of the group to speak out. As described in chapter two, this is the "forming" stage of the group, and it is very important that everyone be included. It is the moderator's responsibility to involve everyone at this stage, usually by going around the room, having each person introduce themselves in turn. By asking them, for example, to describe briefly the extent and nature of their library use, the moderator and the group participants can get a sense of who they are and of their experience level. Since this exercise allows participants to talk about themselves, a subject that they obviously know the most about, it makes for easy practice in speaking out in front of the group. If anyone in the group answers very briefly at this stage, it is a good opportunity for the moderator to probe for more information. This shows right at the outset that the moderator is interested in more than just a superficial reply [5]. It can send a reassuring message to the group that they really are here to be listened to, and it shows the shy or less committed participants that they will be challenged to fully involve themselves in the discussion.

Once the ice has been broken, it is important to keep up the momentum by moving directly into the first questions, which are usually fairly general in nature. In our example of the electronic journal discussion, the group might first be asked to describe which journals they have used and where they usually had access to them. If participants have been selected for this focus group because they have some experience with such resources, everyone should have something to say. Hesitancy at this point, therefore, can indicate that there are individuals who may be generally less inclined to speak out and might need special encouragement as the discussion continues. It can also identify those who may need to be kept in check because they are repetitive, stray from the topic, or simply tend to monopolize the conversation. Such early indications can be very useful for the moderator in learning how to manage group members.

Even though there is no logical reason for anyone not to respond at this point, many people may still be hesitant to speak out until they get a better feel for how the group "works." The first moments of any focus group discussion can therefore be full of silences while group members get used to their role. It is important that the moderator appear relaxed and unhurried during this time. Rushing into the void with more questions can only cause confusion. When someone does offer a comment or opinion, the moderator should not immediately offer their own viewpoint in return but rather encourage others to respond. This will demonstrate the moderator's willingness to listen and that he or she is comfortable with silence while people put together their responses. Such an atmosphere of listening rather than questioning will encourage people to speak out, which is of course the whole point of the exercise. Similarly, it is important that the moderator never come across as being judgmental; that neither agreement or disagreement with what is said be shown; and that all comments are seen as being taken equally seriously.

Focusing the Discussion: Now that the real discussion has begun, it is time for the moderator to lead into the key questions that will gather the opinions needed to meet the goals of the focus group project. While encouraging spontaneous discussion and the expression of different points of view, the moderator must also make sure that participants stay focused on the topic and the specific question under discussion. Conversations can easily be side-tracked, especially when participants feel strongly about an issue. Only by paying close attention to what is being said can the moderator recognize when the conversation is going off track. If group members do begin to digress, by picking up some reference or allusion in their remarks and relating it back to the topic, the moderator can help get the discussion back on track with a well-placed comment or question to a participant [6].

A good moderator, however, will recognize when such discussions might open up useful new insights that had not been anticipated during question development. In the earlier example, misconceptions regarding the cost of electronic journals or unanticipated fears that access to printed journals would be eliminated might not have been expected by the library. Either of these could greatly color the opinions of a potential but unconvinced user, about the electronic medium. This emphasizes the importance of having the moderator closely involved in the initial planning for the focus group. In order to successfully lead the group, the moderator must be very clear on the library's objectives in holding the discussion and on the specific goals of the focus group itself. Only in this way can the moderator know when to redirect the discussion and when to allow it to be at least somewhat diverted.

Discussion Techniques: Because the major objective of a focus group is to have each member respond to each topic introduced, the moderator may be called upon to use many different techniques during this central phase of the focus group project. There is need to keep the discussion focused on the key questions. The simplest technique to do this is often silence, which both allows thought and signals that the moderator is not yet "done" with this topic. While it seems easy to achieve, silence can in fact be difficult to deal with. Especially for new moderators, the tendency is to try to fill gaps in the conversation to keep the discussion alive. In fact, silences usually play an important role in any conversation. By remaining quiet after each new question is asked, the moderator allows group members to formulate their answers and respond thoughtfully and, more importantly, in their own words. Then, once a comment has been made, a further pause on the part of the moderator encourages other members to respond either in agreement, or with a different point of view. Not only does silence draw out additional opinions and comments, it also encourages participants to interact with one another rather than just with the moderator. Since the information generated by such group interaction is one of the major benefits of a focus group, it is clearly important for the moderator to recognize when and how to use pauses in the conversation to actually advance it.

While silences can be helpful in the discussion, the moderator must also know when to end them. When it is clear that everyone with something to say on a particular topic has had the opportunity to speak, if there are still individuals who have not volunteered opinions, the moderator should then rejoin the conversation. Repeating the question and asking, for example, how the rest of the group feels about the topic, whether or not they agree with what has been said, or if someone has a different experience or opinion, can encourage those who have been silent. This is especially important for those who have kept quiet because they do not agree with what has been said. Even though the moderator may have emphasized the importance of bringing out different opinions, it is important to reinforce the message that all viewpoints are encouraged and that there are no "right answers." If these techniques still do not succeed in drawing everyone out, sometimes rephrasing the question can be helpful. It may also be necessary, on occasion, to directly question a participant by name. However, the moderator must recognize and acknowledge when the group really has no more to say on a topic, or that a particular subject seems unimportant to them, and help them move on to another specific question or concept.

If the group is responsive and outspoken once the discussion is underway, the moderator may simply be able to introduce each new question and, without much encouragement, let the group take over. In some groups, even this amount of moderator involvement may be unnecessary and the discussion will spontaneously flow along the lines described by the moderator in the introduction. Whatever the degree of involvement, the moderator should always be aware of how much individual members are participating, and intervene when necessary to make sure that everyone is included. Quieter members may need much more encouragement to speak out. This can be accomplished by simply paying more attention to them, and acknowledging even their slightest input. While a good moderator is able to project interest and enthusiasm for everyone's contributions, it is particularly important to do this for the less responsive individuals. Sometimes, however, the moderator may need to be more active by, for example, calling on these individuals directly. This is best done when a new topic is introduced rather than at the end of a discussion in which they have shown little interest. If someone is approached directly, it is more successful to ask an unstructured question, which encourages them to draw on their own experience, for example, "What were your thoughts about . . . ?" than to ask a very specific, direct question [7]. Another way to encourage unresponsive individuals, or even whole groups, is with the use of various projective techniques. Sentence completion, free association, drawing pictures, or role playing can all help to stimulate discussion [8]. While these are often used in marketing research, they may not always be appropriate in the library setting and either a librarian moderator or the group may be inexperienced or unresponsive in their use. They can, however, be kept as a fall-back technique if the moderator feels comfortable using them. Finally, if all else fails, and the topic is particularly important, the moderator can simply go systematically around the group, talking to each member individually. While this does force everyone to speak, it cannot guarantee that the views expressed are spontaneous or even genuine, since the tendency for people is to agree with what they have heard if they have no real opinion themselves. If this appears to be the case, the moderator can attempt to verify what appears to be merely a repetition of someone else's opinion by asking the respondent to elaborate further. Questioning individual responses in this way can draw out reticent group members and get a better sense of how they really feel about a particular issue. However, this technique must always be used carefully because there is a danger that anyone challenged in this way might feel intimidated or that the trusting atmosphere of the group might be threatened.

Encouraging full discussion in a focus group can also mean restraining the more dominant talkers if they begin to monopolize the discussion. If such people are allowed to take over the group, not only are other opinions not heard, participants come to expect that domination, and wait for the individual to respond after each new topic is introduced. This can inhibit spontaneity and skew the direction of the discussion, since participants will be reacting to the individual more than to the overall topic. Such situations can be difficult to deal with. Clearly the moderator does not want to offend anyone or stifle potential contributions, yet some type of intervention is necessary to maintain the integrity of the process and ultimately the success of the discussion. Wells refers to this as "pest control" and suggests various coping strategies [9]. In such situations, the moderator should handle the individual firmly but diplomatically. Avoiding eye contact or looking bored, asking pointedly for other people's views, or, if necessary, interrupting, can all be used successfully. If someone must be interrupted, it is helpful to assure him or her that while the group will get back to what they were saying, it is time to hear from someone else who may have a different opinion. This will send a message not only to the individual, that domination is not acceptable, but also to the group, that differing viewpoints are encouraged and everyone's opinion is of equal importance. It is important, however, for the moderator to feel comfortable in using whatever technique seems most appropriate, and to balance the needs and comfort level of the individual with the well being of the group in general.

Whatever the overall nature of the group, responsive or quiet, most individuals need at least some encouragement to speak out and expand their answers sufficiently so that others will understand them and be able to respond. While in general, moderators should try to keep a low profile during the discussion so that participants will use their own words and not be led in any particular direction in their responses, some simple prompts can help keep the conversation flowing without unduly influencing the content. For example, raising one's eyebrows at the end of someone's conversation is a universally recognized method of encouraging further talk. The action does not signify agreement or disagreement, but it seems to demand further explanation. This is an easy and neutral technique for the moderator to use. McCracken suggests various other prompts, including the repetition, in an interrogative tone, of a key term used in a participant's last remark [10]. This questioning of some important word or phrase, usually draws out the speaker, again without signifying whether or not the moderator agrees with the remark.

Beyond employing these simple techniques, which are relatively easy to use and do not interrupt the flow of conversation, the moderator may sometimes need to use more obtrusive methods. "Probing" is one of the more common methods used in focus groups to help participants expand on their opinions or clarify vague responses. Probes can also help get at the reasons behind participant's responses. Sentences such as: "Would you explain that further?", or, "Would you give me an example of what you mean?" are simple but effective probes [11]. This type of wording is specific enough to help individuals further explain what they are trying to say. But it is also neutral enough that they do not feel their views are being questioned or criticized, and must be defended. Likewise, by responding to someone's statement with, "How did you feel about that?" or "Why did you do that?" [12], or by reacting to someone's non-verbal behavior with a comment such as, "I see you shaking your head!" [13], the moderator can help reveal underlying reasons or rationale and enrich the overall results.

Using these techniques can increase the productivity of any focus group, and they are generally easy for even a first-time moderator to employ. Just as important is the creation and maintenance of a friendly, non-critical and open atmosphere in which all comments are welcome, and no one's answer is "wrong." Moderators can encourage the development of this type of atmosphere by building a warm and genuine rapport with the group. There are various techniques available to help with this, such as mirroring, in which the moderator adopts the posture or body language of the group, or even reflects their choice of words and manner of speech. New moderators should be careful when attempting to use these techniques, since if they are not carried out successfully they can appear to be rude. However, some degree of mirroring is a natural, nearly spontaneous adaptation to even simple normal conversations. We all learn to adapt our voice and behavior to a specific situation in which interpersonal interactions occur.

An easier method for building rapport perhaps, is through trading disclosures. If, for instance, someone has a problem using computers, by admitting their own fears when first using such equipment, moderators can encourage these individuals to talk more freely about their experiences. Another type of disclosure is admitting ignorance or confusion. If someone makes an unclear statement or introduces an unknown topic, the moderator should not hesitate to admit a lack of knowledge, and ask for clarification. New moderators might even admit that it is their first focus group. Such admissions can help develop a warmer relationship with group members, and signal to them that it is acceptable to admit ignorance or uncertainty. Again, this is a common and casual action for most good conversationalists.

Even in the best run focus groups things can go wrong. Apart from problems with the over-talkative or the silent member, some moderators may experience a participant who tries to take over and lead the group into another topic. Although the moderator does not want to dominate the group, there is a specific purpose for the discussion and it is important to remind the group of that purpose. Another problem is having two members who constantly disagree with one another. Especially if they also tend to be outspoken and talkative, this can become very disruptive. To resolve this, the moderator might want to involve other members of the group by asking how they feel about this constant disagreement. Sometimes, by publicly recognizing that a problem exists, the group may be able to resolve it, and at the same time, expand the discussion. Reminding people that differences are OK can also serve to diffuse an otherwise potentially difficult situation. Finally, a group which has been generally talkative and interactive, can sometimes freeze at a particular topic or point in the discussion. Again, the moderator can intervene, either by introducing laughter or some other different stimulation to raise energy level, or by acknowledging the problem and asking the group to discuss the situation.

Once all the main questions have been asked, the final step is to bring closure to the discussion. This can be accomplished in a number of ways. A relatively simple approach is for the moderator to provide a brief review of the purpose of the discussion and ask for any additional comments. Hearing once again why the group has been brought together, can sometimes trigger a new thought or insight in the participants. Another useful strategy, if there is time, is for the moderator to have each member of the group sum up their own feelings about the general topic and add anything they may have wanted to say earlier. This is a good opportunity for people to bring up views that had not been expressed before or to change their minds and retract previous statements, based on what they have subsequently heard and thought about. These late comments can sometimes provide additional valuable information. Indeed, it is possible that individuals who have been reluctant to speak out earlier, for whatever reason, may take this last chance to get their point across. Those who are timid about airing controversial views or reluctant to express differing opinions from others in the group may see this as an opportunity to speak out without being challenged or contradicted because of the lack of time.

If there is not sufficient time for everyone to participate individually in this summarization, it can still be useful for the moderator to provide a summary of the key points of the discussion and ask participants if they agree with this perception. This is especially true for issues that inspired heated or lengthy discussion; the moderator must have a good sense of whether all members feel equally strongly or if there is general agreement [14]. This is a time when it is especially important for the moderator to look for non-verbal clues from the participants. Any signs of disagreement, hesitation, or concern should be probed so that different views are expressed and clarified. This summarization also allows the moderator to begin to formulate the hypotheses and conclusions that will be discussed in the final analysis and reporting of the group. Articulating these ideas to the group can help validate the conclusions drawn by the moderator [15]. A final alternative is to have the moderator ask participants if they felt anything had been missed in the discussion which the library should be made aware of. This can also bring out new and useful information and may sometimes open up a new line of discussion.

Whatever technique is used to end the discussion, it is important for some type of formal closure to be made, not just for the sake of any new information gathered, but also for the satisfaction of the participants.

Individuals who feel that their time has been well spent will be more likely and willing to attend future groups and will perhaps encourage their friends and colleagues also to get involved. The moderator should take this last opportunity to again thank the group members for taking time to attend and for offering their valuable insights and opinions, and to assure them that the library will seriously consider their views. Library focus groups depend on the willingness of users to participate fully and honestly in telling the library what is on their minds. It is important that moderators realize the critical nature of the participants' contributions and make the focus group experience as satisfying and productive as possible.

REFERENCES

1. Krueger RA. Focus groups: a practical guide for applied research. 2nd ed. Thousand Oaks, CA: Sage, 1994:112.
2. O'Donnell JM. Focus groups: a habit forming evaluation technique. Train & Dev J, 1988 Jul; 42(7):71–3.
3. Gordon W, Langmaid R. Qualitative market research: a practitioner's and buyer's guide. Aldershot, England: Gower, c1988:53.
4. Wells WD. Group interviewing. In: Ferber R., ed. Handbook of marketing research. New York: McGraw Hill, 1974:2–139.
5. *Ibid.*, 2–140.
6. Merton RK, Fiske M, Kendall PL. The focused interview: a manual of problems and procedures. 2nd ed. New York: Macmillan, 1990:154.
7. *Ibid.*, 157.
8. Advertising Research Foundation. Focus groups: issues and approaches. New York: The Foundation, 1985:14.
9. Wells, op cit., 2–142.
10. McCracken G. The long interview. Newbury Park, CA: Sage Publications, 1988:35.
11. Krueger, op. cit., 116.
12. Holloway I, Wheeler S. Qualitative research for nurses. Oxford, England: Blackwell Scientific, 1996:58.
13. Vaughn S, Schumm JS, Sinagub J. Focus group interviews in education and psychology. Thousand Oaks, CA: Sage Publications, 1996:81.
14. *Ibid.*, 46–7.
15. Debus M. Methodological review: a handbook for excellence in focus group research. Washington, DC: Porter Novelli, 1988:42.

10

The Final Steps: Analysis, Reporting, and Use of the Results

·᷾ᴸ·

Conducting a focus group discussion on any subject generates a large amount of data, usually in the form of audiotapes of the discussion and written notes taken by an observer or assistant moderator, if one is used. These are the raw data from which an analysis is made in order to understand the content of the discussion and prepare a report of the results and conclusions. But like most conversations, these raw data are likely to be disorganized, somewhat repetitive or contradictory, and expressed in different terms and contexts. To be useful, the ideas expressed in the group must be organized, and condensed and analyzed.

The process of analysis is essentially made up of two elements: mechanical and intellectual. The mechanical part involves organization of the data, through "cutting and pasting," into units of information such as phrases, sentences, etc., followed by grouping of those units into categories that represent the major concepts in the discussion. The intellectual part covers the determination of what constitutes a unit, a category, or subcategory into which the data are organized, and the review of each category to draw overall conclusions. Reporting the results can be through a written document or an oral presentation. Table 10–1 outlines the steps which make up the analysis process.

Table 10–1

Steps in Focus Group Data Analysis

- Hold debriefing session to record impressions and review observer's notes
- Transcribe discussion tapes
- Review tapes to correct transcript and include debriefing/observer notes
- Determine topic categories for data coding
- Decide on coding system to be used
- Review complete transcript and code data
- Re-arrange data into categories
- Review and analyze each category for interpretation
- Prepare report

Ideally, it is the moderator who plays the part of analyst and reporter. This individual has been involved with the project from the beginning, was the key to the discussion itself, and is almost always best aware of the nuances behind the transcribed words. He or she is thus likely to be the most capable person for reviewing and categorizing the data, and interpreting and reporting the results. In this stage of the focus group project, all the information gathered is important: both the actual statements made and their tone and emphasis, as well as any other behavioral or non-verbal clues that can affect the interpretation of the discussion. If multiple focus groups are utilized, transcripts, notes, and observations from all the group meetings should be collated and analyzed, in order to develop an overall picture of the discussions and to increase the amount of information gathered and validate the results.

The analysis phase of the focus group process has been characterized by some researchers as the most challenging [1]. It requires both knowledge of the topics and judgment and analysis of multiple responses as well as simpler organizing skills for handling and rearranging data. Unlike the analysis of quantitative data where statistical methods apply, working with qualitative research results is much less standardized and clearly defined. One result of this is an abundance of literature on the topic of qualitative analysis, including general guides such as Miles and Huberman's sourcebook [2], and a host of more specific works aimed at various disciplines in the social and behavioral sciences. In spite of the large number of sources, few of them provide practical details on what has been called the "nuts and bolts" of the actual analysis [3]. Because of this, they can be confusing, even overwhelming to the librarian researcher with little experience in formal research methods. Library staff may not have the time or skills to attempt complex analysis following these methods, nor is this likely to be necessary for most focus group projects. Unfortunately, the literature dealing specifically with focus group data is not much better, because much of it gives little specific guidance for this stage of the research project. Faced with multiple tapes or lengthy transcripts, it may seem an impossible task to reduce all these statements to a coherent and valid interpretation that will provide useful insights. Yet a small amount of experience and organization should show that this is not the case; almost all focus group discussions that have been conducted well can be productively analyzed.

An important point to remember is that analysis should be problem-driven. The original purpose of the project should be the guide to determining just how much detail is needed and what techniques should be used. Even the issue of whether or not to transcribe the tapes of the sessions should be taken into this consideration. Some projects can be successfully completed without a full transcription. Careful listening to the tape, reading the observer notes, and discussing the sessions with other team members, may be sufficient to identify the major themes. Then by reviewing the data again, the analyst can seek out pertinent quotations and notes to support these themes. Having a second person reexamine the data can provide useful validation.

By returning to the reason for the project, it should become apparent whether or not an elaborate or detailed analysis is needed. If the focus groups were held in order to answer a simple problem—for example, should the library revise its opening hours?—then the analysis should answer just that question. Participants may have spent considerable time in "warming up" with introductory comments and general discussion about the library, and all of this will be recorded on the tape. While these preliminaries are extremely important in terms of developing a good group relationship and encouraging participants to speak freely, this section of the discussion may not need to be transcribed nor analyzed closely to answer the simple type of question posed in the example. If, on the other hand, the discussion sought answers to a more complex problem, such as the design of a new end-user training plan, a more elaborate and wide-ranging analysis would be appropriate. Knowing the background of the participants and their pattern of library use can be important factors in developing a successful program. Whatever the complexity of the question, it is important for the library to weigh the resources available (time, staff, money) for the analysis against the value and use of the information to be obtained in return for the effort.

Principles of Analysis: The importance of relating analysis to purpose is one of the guiding principles in analyzing the results of a focus group discussion. By turning back to the intent of the project, the analyst will avoid either too-detailed an analysis of trivial facts, or overlooking important data. This emphasizes the importance of a practical approach in which the extent and level of the analysis and interpretation answers only the question asked. Needless attention to minute details of discussion can waste time, and money, while producing little of practical value. Another fundamental principle to keep in mind is that regardless of the method used and the level of detail employed, it is important that any analysis be systematic and verifiable, so that someone else listening to the tapes or reading through the discussion notes would come up with similar conclusions [4]. Such an approach in fact begins at the very start of the project. It involves careful sequencing of questions to gain the maximum insight; complete recording of all data so that everything in the discussion is captured; thorough and careful coding of the data; immediate debriefing of the interviewing team; and verification by participants, through some type of review during or after the discussion. Keeping both of these principles in mind, the focus group results will be both believable and verifiable, while remaining easy to understand and apply. This should appeal to the library wanting to use results to quickly improve a program or service, yet looking for assurance that the innovations will not be a waste of time and money.

If the focus group has been conducted by following these logical steps, the task of analyzing the transcripts and notes can be less arduous. Careful and thoughtful planning will almost always pay off at this stage of the project. However, it is important not to underestimate the time needed for this analysis. A thorough review of all information gathered from the group is another basic principle and surely necessary in the analysis of any library focus group. Only by reviewing the entire transcript or tape can the full meaning of a discussion emerge and the irrelevant data be identified. Selecting only a few comments about a topic on which to base interpretation is misleading, especially because the comments chosen could easily tend to be those that confirm existing points of view of the moderator or library administration. Even if the focus group project was developed to study a single issue, every comment is potentially important. After all, one of the major purposes of the analysis is to raise the level of understanding of the topic under discussion. While focus groups results often reinforce what had been previously suspected, they can also lead to surprises; careful consideration of the whole transcript will allow the new and unpredictable to emerge. This is one of the most valuable and important characteristics of the focus group, and it is only possible because of the open nature of the technique.

As well as devoting sufficient time to analyzing the data, a further principle of focus group analysis is to conduct the analysis soon after the first discussion has been concluded. Delays between convening the group and analyzing the results can have negative consequences, especially if several groups are brought together as part of the overall project. It is hard enough to remember all the impressions and insights resulting from a single focus group. When more than one group is convened in a short period, it becomes almost impossible to differentiate between what happened at the various interviews. Moving quickly into the analysis phase while the discussion is fresh in the minds of the moderator and anyone else involved in conducting the discussion ensures that the overall sense of each group experience is captured and that any non-verbal clues are recorded and subsequently included in the final analysis. Indeed it has been argued that in this type of research methodology, analysis and collection of qualitative data must go hand in hand; that interpretation should in fact begin with the first data gathered [5]. In this way, what is learned from the first discussion can be used to modify the project by reformulating subsequent questions to correct errors or sources of bias, clarify aspects of the discussion, or pursue new avenues of interest which emerge.

Debriefing Sessions: Because of the importance of minimizing delay between the discussions and analyzing the results, a useful preliminary step, before the formal data analysis, is to conduct a debriefing meeting of those who led and observed the discussion. This meeting should be held immediately after the focus group disbands. On a very practical level, the debriefing meeting allows the project team members to make a spot check of the tape to ensure that all the discussion has been recorded. If there are problems with any part of the tape, it is important to reconstruct as much of the missing discussion as possible. Obviously this will be much easier to do immediately rather than if days or weeks elapse after the discussion is over. The debriefing also provides an opportunity for the individuals involved to compare notes and exchange observations. This exchange can help focus on key findings from the discussion and any highlights that may be helpful during the analysis of the tapes. This might include, for example, a particular interaction between participants which became very productive, or, on the other hand, a blind alley in the discussion which lost time and which the moderator will want to avoid with another group. It can also include a consideration of the choice of words by participants to describe certain topics, how consistent people's responses were, whether or not they changed their minds and why. All these can be important data for analysis.

The debriefing discussion can also reveal things that may not have been picked up on tape or even in the written notes. For example, if participants showed enthusiasm for a particular topic, or appeared bored and disinterested in another, this may have been revealed more by body language than by the actual conversation. People's facial expressions can be a valuable clue to what they are really feeling and may be at odds with what they actually say. Interpersonal relationships may be another factor that can influence the discussion yet not be recorded. This could include, for example, the behavior of the group toward a certain individual who might perhaps be someone in a position of authority or a negative relationship between two participants. These types of relationships may influence the discussion by inhibiting free expression or encouraging argument. Yet because they remain largely unspoken, their existence will not necessarily be picked up in the tape recording. The debriefing session is a good opportunity to recognize such interactions and record them so that they can be taken into account during the analysis of the tapes. Professional focus group organizations often use videotape to record these visual clues, but it is unlikely that the library will have the facilities for unobtrusive video recording (one-way mirrors for observation from an adjoining room, recording equipment, etc.). Hence, the fresh memories of the moderator and observers must serve this function.

The debriefing is also an opportunity to review the process of the discussion and see if any changes are needed in future groups. It may become clear that the order of the questions was not appropriate or that a particular question was unclear and needed rewording. Only by reviewing what took place while memories are fresh can this type of insight and understanding be reached. As mentioned earlier, while the information from this debriefing can be useful in practical terms, for improving the next group discussion, it is in fact an integral part of the final analysis. The notes made during this debriefing session should therefore be provided to whoever is analyzing the rest of the focus group data.

Qualitative Analysis: The formal, qualitative analysis of the discussion usually begins by listening to the tape, reviewing the transcripts, and reading notes from the observer and from the debriefing meeting. Although it may be easier and faster to work just from the transcript, there are drawbacks to using just this method. In the transcript, much of the feeling of the discussion is lost and errors can creep in. It is difficult for the individual transcribing the tape to make sense of the discussion when more than one person is talking at once, or if someone is speaking quickly. This is especially true if the transcriber was not present at the discussion and so has no personal memories of the event. No matter how good the moderator might have been, garbled sections of the transcript are inevitable as the group gets caught up in their discussion. If the transcriber was not present during the actual meeting of the group, some comments or threads of ideas can be completely missed. Also missing from a transcript are the emotions that are present. A written document cannot easily reveal if someone sounds very enthusiastic, fearful, or doubtful. For example, interpreting a statement such as "I like it" can be difficult because this might be a strong conviction or just a polite response [6]. Transcripts do provide easy access to the discussion and, if the moderator is doing the analysis, he or she is likely to remember the tone and manner of each respondent provided that the discussion did not occur too far in the past. Probably the most practical solution is for the analyst to read through the transcript and then go back and listen to the tapes to "fill in" nuances and intensities of feeling, and annotate the transcript appropriately.

Because the transcript will become the working document for further analysis, it is important, during this review of the tapes, to make any necessary corrections or omissions on the written document. Once the analyst feels that the transcript is a fair and accurate depiction of what was said and, where necessary, how it was said, the next step is to review the notes from the debriefing and any that were taken during the group meeting. From these the analyst is able to understand the more subtle, non-verbal aspects of the group interchange that were observed during the discussion and that are usually not captured on the tape. Since these can influence how people respond and affect the flow of the discussion, they can be important keys to interpretation. By reviewing not just what was said but how it was said and how the group reacted, a more complete understanding of the entire group interchange is possible. Adding this supplemental information to appropriate portions of the transcript will reflect these non-verbal aspects, and ensure their consideration in the final analysis.

Although the preceding steps may take considerable time to accomplish, the end result will be a complete and accurate set of notes that capture the whole focus group experience. Wagner and Mahmoodi stress the importance of having notes that will allow the analyst, among other things, to trace a particular idea throughout the whole discussion; identify either a person or a subgroup to whom a particular idea is important; and separate out ideas that belong to individuals as opposed to the group as a whole [7].

Segmenting the Data: A major first step in organizing and interpreting the data is the division of the transcript into meaningful units or segments. Each unit, by definition, contains a single piece of information: an idea, an opinion, etc., that makes sense by itself [8].

These units can be made up of as little as a few words or an entire paragraph. The following example, from a discussion on practicing dentists use of information resources, may help to clarify what makes up a meaningful segment.

> MODERATOR: What is the first source of information you go to when you have a question about a patient?
>
> PRACTITIONER: I've got a computer in my office but it's really just used for billing and word-processing. I don't use it; it's really for my secretary. I don't think about using it for information. I usually call a colleague. You know the difference between calling a colleague and looking through a computer is that there is some wisdom in the colleague and they can do screening for you. You give them one or two words and they respond in an intelligent way as opposed to the way a computer does. I've tried using MEDLINE but haven't had much luck. You put a few key words in and you get everything under the sun!

There are several meaningful segments in this exchange, though not all of them are relevant to the specific question being asked. A segment such as "I've got a computer in my office . . . I don't think about using it for information. I usually call a colleague" makes sense on its own, even when taken out of context, and clearly refers to the question asked. The sentence, "I don't use it; it's really for my secretary," however, is not a meaningful segment since it does not make sense by itself. On the other hand, "I've got a computer in my office but it's really just used for billing and word-processing. I don't use it; it's really for my secretary" while it is meaningful and conveys the idea of the computer's use in the office, is not relevant to the specific question being asked here. It is does, however, pertain to the question of practitioners' access and attitudes toward computers. Likewise, the comment starting, "You know the difference . . ." and ending with the problem of getting "everything under the sun!" also constitutes a meaningful segment, describing the reason this practitioner does not use computers for finding information. Segments, or units, then, should be able to retain their meaning even when they are pulled out of their immediate context. They will not necessarily be nicely organized into successive topics within the transcript of the discussion but may jump back and forth. And they may or may not even be pertinent to the overall discussion.

Determining Categories: The whole point of breaking down the text into discrete, meaningful segments is to be able to rearrange them into categories or clusters. The categories provide a system of organization for the data, which allows comments about each topic to be brought together, so that the analyst can determine everything that was said by the group about each issue discussed and is able to draw conclusions. Determining these categories is another important intellectual challenge in the analysis and there are two major approaches in qualitative data analysis, although in practice researchers often combine the two. In one approach, the researcher creates the categories before the analysis begins, basing them on the overall framework and goals of the focus group project; in effect, using the questions asked to provide the categories. The alternative approach looks to the data themselves to provide the categories, avoiding any prior ideas or expectations about the organization. This approach is common in studies that are open and exploratory in nature, where there are no preconceived hypotheses. For many librarians conducting their first focus group project, the former method will usually be more appropriate since their goals will be quite specific. However, because focus group discussions frequently bring out new and unexpected data, which can make valuable contributions to the project, it is important during the analysis to be continually alert to the possibility of new topics and new categories that arise from reviewing the transcript. This process of determining categories has in fact been likened to indexing a book or deciding on the headings to be used in a filing system [9].

In the above example used to illustrate meaningful segments, the library staff might have decided that they were interested in learning, among other things, about the dentists' choice of information sources, the availability of computers to practitioners, their attitudes toward computers, their frequency of computer use, and reasons for non-use. These, then, would be logical categories for dividing up the textual segments. Because focus group discussions are largely unstructured and spontaneous, the data produced are not usually well organized, even when the questions have been logically introduced and the moderator has exerted some control over the course of the discussion. Unlike quantitative data gathered through an instrument such as a questionnaire, there are no rigidly predefined categories of responses for focus groups. Thus, the job of the analyst at this stage is to examine the entire transcript, determine the relevant units of information, and decide into which category they belong, no matter where in the text the units may appear.

Sorting the Data: Once the categories have been determined, it is helpful to make a list of them to refer to while reviewing the transcript. With a good list of clearly defined categories, the analyst should have relatively few difficulties in deciding where each unit belongs. Finding relevant sections that do not fit into one of the listed categories may demonstrate the need for creating new categories, or they may be relegated to a "miscellaneous" category for further review later. However, it is important to remember that not all of the text need be marked and categorized. Some comments, just as in any conversation, are simply irrelevant. Experience will help the analyst determine more easily and quickly just what can be ignored. Table 10–2 shows a portion of a transcript, which has been marked up and coded, using simple descriptive phrases for codes.

As the analyst reviews the transcript, the major task is to tag the textual units by some method that will show to which category or categories each one belongs. This process is usually known as coding and may be as simple as using different colored markers, or as complex as developing mnemonic labels that represent both the topic discussed and the place in the transcript where it appeared. Especially for the beginning analyst a simple method such as the use of different colored marking pens for each topic can be quite effective. In the dental practitioner discussion, for example, the topic "availability of computers" might be coded in blue, "attitudes toward computers" in red, "frequency of computer use" in green, and "reasons for non-use" in black. A key to the colors used, along with the definition of each color, would then serve as a guide to the analyst. Then, in reading through the notes, each piece of information pertaining to availability of computers would be either underlined or highlighted in blue, while anything bearing on attitudes toward computers would be colored in red, and so on. While much of the discussion of an issue would follow the posing of the question related to it, relevant comments might be made at any time and so be interspersed throughout the notes. In our example, during a discussion of which resources practitioners use, comments were made about other important topics, including computer attitudes and reasons for non-use, and even briefly touched on problems with searching strategies. Single comments may thus need to be coded in multiple colors since they are applicable to multiple topics.

TABLE 10–2

CODED TRANSCRIPT FROM A FOCUS GROUP DISCUSSION

SPEAKER A: I think we have to remember that **the computer is not going to think for you; the computer is very fast but it's also very stupid and it requires that you, the intelligent questioner, understand what the computer can do for you and what it can't do for you** [*Attitude toward computers*]. People think the computer is going to answer everything and they view it as a superior brain than their own, and they don't understand that it doesn't have a superior brain. It has a brain that is greatly inferior to theirs. It only does things faster.

SPEAKER B: Yeah, and when people look at these online books or other types of information, you know they don't ever go to the bottom of the page and look at the date the thing was written! **They think because it's on the computer that it has to be the latest. Some of the things you are looking at are at least ten years old and that can make a big difference. People just don't stop to think; they accept what's there on the computer as the latest and the best** [*Attitude toward computers*].

SPEAKER C: I agree, they seem to be very accepting, or maybe it's just laziness. . . . they have the information in one place that's convenient, and they don't bother to go anywhere else. But you can sort of understand it; **it would be great if everything was right there, on your computer, in your office and you didn't have to go anywhere else** [*Information need*] . . . the trouble is when I do try to search on the computer, like when I try to search MEDLINE, I usually **end up getting so much that is gobbledy-goop and doesn't seem to be related to what I asked for!!** [*Information seeking behavior*]. . . . **When I do get something interesting I only get a brief description when what I really want is the whole article** [*Information need*].

SPEAKER A: You know that you can do that now **if you have access to the Internet . . . there are millions of whole journals available now and most of them are free.** [*View of Internet as information source*].

SPEAKER C: I don't think they are all free. I've done a bit of searching on the Internet at home and **when I find one of those journals it usually says, stop, you've got to pay for a copy . . . . I don't think that's much of a service** [*View of the Internet/Attitude toward payment for information*].

> SPEAKER D: Well at least you were able to find the journals. . .all I seem to be able to get is advertising. **It's a real pain to have to go through all that searching and not get what you want. . . . I find I waste an incredible amount of time** [*View of the Internet/Information seeking behavior*], and since **I usually do it at home** [*Information seeking behavior*—**would need to include more of the text to make this a whole, understandable comment**], that's supposed to be my time off!

While colored marks can work with a relatively simple transcript, it may not be effective with a more complex discussion. Using actual labels, or codes, for each relevant information unit is another method for marking and organizing data. Any code used must be clearly defined so that it is applied consistently, with a naming scheme that is close to the concept it describes. In our example, a code for the topic of attitude toward computers could be simply ATT-PC or a short phrase such as "ATTITUDES-COMPUTERS," while FREQ-PC or "FREQUENCY-USE" could represent the topic of frequency of use. While codes will largely correspond to the topics covered in the questions, other issues will develop from the discussion which were not foreseen. Since these can often represent important new information, they must also be labeled and included in the final analysis. If codes are to be used, it can be helpful to include wide margins in the transcript sheets where the codes can be written next to the appropriate units of information. Again, it is helpful to have a list of the codes used so that they can be quickly referred to by the analyst.

Once the transcript has been divided into specific units of information and these have been labeled in some manner to indicate their appropriate category, all the units must now be sorted into those categories or "piles" that represent the major themes of the discussion. If notes have been made by the moderator or observer on any particular parts of the transcript, which characterize them in some way, comments on tone of voice, vehemence, etc., these should remain with the appropriate parts. With a simple system, such as color-coding, the transcript can literally be cut up, and the different colored sections sorted into appropriate piles. If the transcript is relatively short and the topics limited, a good alternative is to use a word-processor to cut-and-paste the labeled sections. With more complex coding systems, especially when used with lengthy and/or numerous transcripts, this can be more of a challenge. For this reason, qualitative researchers frequently rely on computers to help them keep track of data during the analysis stage.

Computers in Data Analysis: The process of coding and categorizing qualitative data is clearly time-consuming and exacting. Many researchers routinely use computers in their qualitative projects to help with a number of steps in the analysis process [10]. There are several types of programs available; some were not originally written for data analysis, while others have been developed specifically by individual researchers for their own immediate needs and have subsequently enjoyed a wider utility. General purpose word-processing software, is a good example of the former type of program. Word-processing software is obviously very useful for the preparatory aspects of analysis: data input and transcript correction, numbering lines of text for locating information, moving text into categories, and, in general, conveniently storing and organizing large amounts of data. Because of certain features, such as "search and retrieval," the software can also be used to search the texts for specific words or codes. For library staff, especially when doing their first focus group project, a word-processing program that is familiar and routinely used, is probably the best method for data input and manipulation.

The more specialized programs have other features that can make analysis more efficient. Some of these can organize data more systematically; some can attach codes to segments of the text, search for those codes either singly or in a sequence, and assemble them. A few of them go even further and help with building theories from the data. More than two dozen of these specialized software programs currently exist; although somewhat dated, the information included in Miles and Huberman's work provides a good overview of these packages, along with the names and addresses of their distributors [11]. While these specialized programs can be very helpful and save time in what can be a tedious procedure, their value must be balanced against other factors. Such programs are not generally available in the local software store, and the time involved in acquiring and becoming familiar with them can be considerable. This may not turn out to be an advantage if the focus group methodology and, consequently, the specialized software, are infrequently used by library staff. Whatever method is used, either manual or computer based, to sort and rearrange focus group data, it is a painstaking and sometimes difficult task.

Interpreting the Data: Once the coding is completed and all the data for each objective/category and its various subcategories are brought together, the interpretation can begin. At this point, it is important for the analyst to have a clear understanding of the level of interpretation required by the library manager or other individual requesting the information. Krueger describes a continuum of analysis, which ranges from a simple accumulation of data to a full interpretation [12]. The accumulation approach would simply organize the statements of the participants under each topic, perhaps arranged by some characteristic such as profession (*e.g.*, nurses, physicians, faculty, or students). Because discussions can result in very large amounts of information, however, this may not be very useful to the library. It does provide the library manager with all the available information for making decisions, though perhaps in the form of an indigestible meal!

The middle of this continuum reduces the amount of data presented by providing summary statements of participants on each topic. These summaries can also include some direct quotations, which illustrate either typical responses to a topic or the range of ideas expressed. Such an approach can provide a good sense of the discussion without including every statement made. Clearly this approach means less work on the part of the manager in assimilating the information, however, it reduces the amount of information available for decision making and relies on the skills of the analyst to have included the most pertinent. It is extremely important in preparing these summaries, that the analyst not be too biased or selective, choosing only those comments and quotations that confirm a particular point of view. This can be a danger if the analyst is too closely associated with the focus group project and has a personal stake in the outcome. To be an accurate record of the discussion, summaries must be comprehensive, balanced, and objective.

At the other end of the continuum is the full interpretation, which obviously involves much more work for the analyst but provides the meaning of the data rather than just a summary, and helps in understanding what the group discussion was all about. It is here that the librarian moderator/analyst has the advantage over an outside researcher because of the extensive background knowledge of the library which he or she can bring to this phase of the project. A basic understanding of the library and its users provides authenticity and depth to the interpretation. Such an interpretation will often bring in outside information, from the literature or from other library situations, either as verification or as a comparison with the findings of the project. Recommendations are often included in this type of analysis. Once again, objectivity on the part of the individual responsible for the analysis is essential. The goal of the analysis is to provide an overall understanding of the project's findings and their implications for the library.

In determining the approach to be used for the analysis, the complexity and level of interpretation needed should be dictated by the original purpose of the project and by the data themselves, as well as by the requirements of the individual initiating the project. Some focus group discussions result in very clear patterns of thought, with little difference of opinion on the topics covered. In such cases, interpretation may be very simple and straightforward. Other discussions can move in unexpected directions, reach conclusions that were not previously considered, or involve serious and insoluble disagreements among participants. Practicality should dictate the amount of time and effort put into interpretation, and the original intent of the focus group project must always be kept in mind.

The interpretation itself involves looking for patterns, relationships, and trends among the various comments in order to better understand the problems or issues that are the subject of the focus group project. Concentrating on one issue at a time will ensure that all pertinent information about that issue is considered: not only the participants' comments, but the impressions and nonverbal information taken from the debriefing and observer notes. As all these opinions and ideas about a topic are reviewed and the amount of agreement or disagreement, the strength of feeling, etc., are assessed, conclusions can be formulated. Although the focus group methodology is qualitative, it is legitimate to include in the analysis a sense of how much or little agreement there is among participants on specific issues. Such information is not used to project results onto a larger population, it merely gives a sense of the group as a whole. Other groups might lead to a different degree of agreement or even a different conclusion, depending on their character. But in any instance conclusions are not based on a single person's opinions; rather they come from a complete review of the topic as revealed through the entire discussion. Since opinions can be changed in the group environment, the analyst should also trace the flow of the discussion through the entire transcript in order to understand those changes and if appropriate, note them in the analysis. Whatever conclusions are reached, it is important to show the rationale leading up to them. This can be done through the use of direct quotations or paraphrases, as well as through a description of the progression in thought. For example, an initially negative response to facilities for printing in the library could be shown to become positive with the idea of more printers or new printers being installed, or the possibility of e-mailing output to a personal workstation.

In reviewing the discussion notes, it is also important to keep in mind that what is not said about a topic can also be revealing. This absence of discussion may have several meanings. An obvious one is that the topic is of little importance to the participants. Such a conclusion, however, cannot be taken for granted; any interpretation should always be made within the context of the discussion. If a group, for example, does not mention problems with printing during a discussion of the online catalog, this may be for several reasons: perhaps no one experienced problems because the library's printing arrangements work well. On the other hand, it may be that no one in the group had actually done any printing and therefore had nothing to say, or they had so many difficulties that they no longer even attempt to print the output. Or, perhaps no one thought to talk about printing because there was so much else to discuss. Unless the question about printing was specifically asked, conclusions cannot be drawn because of a lack of discussion on the topic. However, if the discussion makes clear that most of the participants do in fact routinely print from the catalog, it is probably safe to assume that printing is satisfactory and therefore not an issue.

Whatever the approach and degree of analysis that is used, the quality and validity of the final analysis can always be improved through feedback. Co-moderators, observers, or other members of the project can all provide valuable assistance because each will have a somewhat different point of view. Individuals such as observers are particularly helpful; being in the group and listening and observing without the pressure of moderating allows complete attention to the discussion and provides a good insight into the group experience as a whole. Group participants can also supply feedback either by their summaries or by their comments on the moderator's summary at the conclusion of the discussion. It is also possible to send out transcripts or preliminary analyses to group members for their review and comment. Outsiders who are familiar either with the group members, the subject of the discussion, or with qualitative methodologies could also be called on to give different perspectives. Whatever kind of feedback is provided, it is useful to have someone else review the discussion notes and make their own interpretations. This can help validate the analyst's work, add to the understanding of the results, and avoid questions of preconception of results or bias in the analysis.

Reporting Focus Group Findings: The best method used for the interpretation of the focus group discussions is in part determined by what type of report is required. Typically focus group results are presented either as an oral report, a written report, or a combination of the two, depending on the needs of the individual who initiated the project. If a written report is required, this can be in various formats. The Advertising Research Foundation recommends that written reports include:

- a summary of the findings;
- some information on the background and objectives of the study;
- a description of the methodology, including numbers and locations of interviews and characteristics of the participants;
- detailed findings, conclusions and recommendations [13].

Whatever the exact format, it makes sense to use the questions or major objectives of the project as the framework for the report. For each question, it is important to indicate if everyone shared a particular opinion or if only a few felt this way. Although the analyst is primarily looking for information that is repeated by various participants in one group and confirmed by other groups, it is also important to note the range of opinions on a topic, and their variety. Several groups convened to discuss access to information in the library, for example, might all mention their concerns about not being able to find recent journal issues. While this should be highlighted in the project report, other comments about difficulties in finding any type of library materials should also be noted, even though they may be mentioned less frequently, because they might point to a general problem with shelving practices that the library may wish to investigate further. Quotations that are pertinent should also be included, either because they are typical or they present an innovative idea or argument. In selecting quotations to use, it is most helpful to use those that illustrate opinions on the major questions being considered by the study.

Determining whether there are any commonalities among the different topics or within response patterns throughout the entire discussion is also helpful. Do participants react negatively, for example, whenever a particular library service is discussed? Are computers always viewed as a blessing or a nuisance? Do certain categories of users have similar fears or concerns no matter what library service is being discussed? These common threads or patterns of response can be enlightening and provide library staff with additional insight beyond the specific questions investigated by the focus group project. If the project involves discussions with several types of groups, (*e.g.,* physicians, nurses, students), it may be helpful to prepare a global summary in which the findings of each type of group are summarized, and the trends in attitudes, knowledge, etc., are reported. This makes comparisons among the groups possible for each objective. It allows library staff, for example, to see how physicians, nurses, students, etc., differ in their concerns and needs for journal access, working space, library schedules, or computer availability.

Comparison of the focus group project results with existing knowledge or practice in the library is another useful methodology. For example, a library may have a policy of opening early in the morning to allow hospital staff access before their work day officially begins. In analyzing a focus group discussion of service hours, data may reveal that staff in fact prefer to use the library in the evenings. Including in the report a comparison of this finding with the current library practice, can be a helpful way to present the information learned from the study.

Finally, it is helpful to look at the insights gained from the analysis and determine if they suggest the need for further study. While many of the conclusions reached may be obvious, there will be instances when there is no clear cut explanation and alternative explanations may need to be presented. In such cases, especially if the issues are central to the project, further groups may need to be convened that focus just on these issues. Alternatively, it may become apparent that some other method of input such as a survey or individual interviews may need to be used to gather more or different information.

Analyzing and reporting results from a focus group project is a time-consuming activity. The data for analysis: the words, tone of voice, and other non-verbal responses of the group participants, can be voluminous and difficult to organize and work with. The process of analysis—looking for patterns among these words; considering the meaning of the non-verbal aspects of the discussion; and drawing conclusions from everything that is reported—calls for patience and a certain amount of judgment. It is the job of the analyst to use the information gained from this process in order to understand the problems and issues that lie behind the focus group project. Often the results are straightforward: patterns are easy to identify, and there is little difference between the groups or within a particular group. This consistency of opinion can make the conclusions self-evident. Sometimes it is difficult to reach conclusions; many different opinions are expressed and there are no common threads; alternative interpretations must be put forward. Sometimes the project will need to be extended either to further validate what has been learned or to better understand some of the results.

Using the Results: The final step in a focus group project is, of course, the use of the information gathered. Clearly the library had a purpose in conducting the study: questions to answer, concerns to address. Hopefully the knowledge gained through analysis of the accumulated data will help to achieve that purpose. What is ultimately done with that knowledge, however, will depend not only on the purpose, but also on the findings themselves. They may result in action or change; new services added, old services revamped. They may merely add to the understanding of user needs or behaviors and result in little or no immediate visible change. Finally, they may have a negative impact, with services dropped or planned activities canceled. Whatever the outcome, it is very important that this information be shared with the library staff. This is especially true if one or two members of the staff have been involved in the project and as a result other staff have taken on additional temporary responsibilities. Knowing what was learned and how that information will be used, can avoid any negative feelings toward either the project or the methodology.

Focus group projects, if they are carefully planned and executed, can provide valuable insight into the topic under investigation. With careful execution and analysis, this type of qualitative methodology can be an efficient way to explore many library-related issues. It is an ideal way for libraries to hear directly from those whom they serve. The final chapter in this book will present two different case studies to illustrate the various aspects of conducting focus group research in the library.

REFERENCES

1. Knodel J. The design and analysis of focus group studies: a practical approach. In: Morgan DL, ed. Successful focus groups: advancing the state of the art. Newbury Park, CA: Sage Publications, 1993:43.
2. Miles MB, Huberman AM. Qualitative data analysis: an expanded source-book. 2d ed. Thousand Oaks, CA: Sage Publications, c1994.
3. Vaughn S, Schumm JS, Sinagub J. Focus group interviews in education and psychology. Thousand Oaks, CA: Sage Publications, 1996.
4. Krueger RA. Focus groups: a practical guide for applied research. 2nd ed. Thousand Oaks, CA: Sage, 1994:129.
5. Holloway I, Wheeler S. Qualitative research for nurses. Oxford: Blackwell Scientific, 1996.

6. Advertising Research Foundation. Focus groups: issues and approaches. New York: The Foundation, 1985:18.
7. Wagner MM, Mahmoodi SH. A focus group interview manual. New York: American Library Association, Continuing Library Education Network and Exchange Round Table, 1994:10.
8. Tesch R. Qualitative research: analysis types and software tools. New York: Falmer Press, 1990:117.
9. Patton, MQ. Qualitative evaluation methods. Beverly Hills, CA: Sage Publications, 1980:299.
10. Weaver A, Atkinson P. Microcomputing and qualitative data analysis. Aldershot, England: Avebury, 1994.
11. Miles, Huberman, op. cit., 311–7.
12. Krueger, op. cit., 131.
13. Advertising Research Foundation, op. cit., 20.

11

CASE STUDIES:
FOCUS GROUPS IN THE LIBRARY

Focus group interviewing is a research methodology that should appeal to libraries of all types and sizes. This book has provided librarians with information and practical guidance so that they can understand the place of the focus group in qualitative research and begin to utilize it in their own institutions. The previous chapters have considered all the important factors in carrying out a focus group project: choosing a moderator, developing questions, selecting participants, creating the right setting, conducting the interview, and analyzing the results. In order to bring those various aspects together, two case studies are presented here, one set in a large, academic health sciences library; the other in a small hospital library. Each case is a fictionalized composite of actual focus group projects.

The Academic Setting: The Visalius University Medical Center library has been awarded a large sum of money by a private philanthropic organization that supports health related research. This money comes with few stipulations other than that it be spent to support the work of a particular independent research institute within the university. The Timson Institute consists of approximately one hundred individuals, including ten faculty members, thirty postdoctoral fellows, thirty graduate students, as well as some office and non-professional support personnel. The library director decides to involve institute members in making the decisions on how to spend the funds. She believes that sending a letter or even a questionnaire to this group may not be very successful either in response rate or in producing practical solutions, which might benefit more than just a single researcher. Hence the decision is made to hold a series of focus groups, and because bringing these individuals together is no small task, the director decides to use the opportunity to learn more about how this group uses the library and how satisfied they are with library and information services.

The decision is made to use the head of the reference department to lead the focus group project and serve as moderator. This individual has been at the library several years, in public service, and is very familiar with all sorts of library patrons. She is outgoing, a good listener, an experienced teacher and group leader, and is interested in developing focus group interviewing skills. She is also seen by the director to be open minded, interested in the welfare of the entire library, and therefore not likely to direct the discussion to favor her own department. A librarian from the learning resources division is selected to assist the project leader. He has attended a focus group and is interested in learning more about the technique. He is felt to be very competent and innovative in technological matters and is aware of the library practices of the research community, but less attuned to the concerns of the other departments of the library. Pulling individuals from two different divisions will avoid putting an undue burden on the staff in any single department in the library. These individuals, together with the director, make up the project team. The director uses the first meeting of the team to discuss, at length, her thoughts and expectations for the project. After some debate, and pooling of questions and impressions about this research community, the team decide on their major objectives for the study:

- To gather suggestions on how best to spend the money in the library to support institute members' research needs;
- To learn more about the information seeking behavior of the members;
- To understand how satisfied members are with current library and information services and resources;
- To learn about possible new services and resources that the library might provide to improve information access to the institute.

As they discuss some aspects of the project and what will be involved, the director offers the services of one of the administrative assistants to help with transcribing interview tapes, and with various arrangements and room set up. She gives the team members a budget, $250, to cover expenses for the entire project. All agree that there should be some inducement to encourage participation and a free meal is decided on, to be held immediately before the discussion. The only other expenses foreseen are for the audiotapes to recording the sessions. Finally, an agreement is reached that at the end of the discussions the team will provide a written report to the library director, which will include summary statements on each question, along with overall recommendations and a copy of the transcripts of the sessions for the director to refer to if she feels this is necessary.

Soon after the initial meeting with the director, the implementation team again meets to develop a plan of action and time-line, assign duties for each member of the team, and decide on all possible expenses so that a more specific budget can be determined. At this time, preliminary questions are drawn up in a rough format, to determine exactly what will be covered in the discussion, and the decision is made to hold three sessions: one just for faculty, and two for post-doctoral fellows and graduate students. A letter is drafted for the head of the Timson Institute, explaining the library's proposed focus group project and introducing the library staff who will be involved. The letter also asks for her assistance in selecting participants. Copies of the letter, plan, timeline, and budget are forwarded to the library director for approval. The letter is subsequently sent out under the signature of the library director.

The team leader follows up this letter with a telephone call to the institute's director and sets up a meeting. During this meeting, the objectives and plan of action for the project are discussed and a list of possible participants is drawn up. At the suggestion of the director, a decision is made to try to include all the faculty in one group, and to hold two mixed sessions for fellows and those graduate students who are within two years of finishing their degrees because they are no longer taking classes but are using the library heavily for research purposes. The director also suggests suitable dates and times for the sessions and warns the team about upcoming seminars and faculty meetings that would be unsuitable times to hold group discussions. She then provides names of some key faculty who might be helpful in suggesting good candidates, from the student population, to attend the discussions. Finally, the director offers the use of the institute's conference room and agrees to mention the project at the next faculty meeting, along with the fact that professors may soon be contacted by the team members.

Following several phone calls to these key faculty members, several of whom are very cooperative in suggesting fellows and students who are articulate and likely to be active discussion members, a complete list of potential participants is drawn up. The faculty members also give suggestions as to good and bad times for the various categories of participants and as a result several tentative dates are selected. Acting on advice from the faculty, the team decides to hold the faculty session at lunch time and provide coffee, soft drinks, and cookies, and to set up two early evening sessions for other institute members, where pizza and soft drinks will be served before the discussions. The team members then begin contacting individuals by telephone and e-mail to briefly explain the project, the role of the participants, the time and place of the sessions, and ask for a specific commitment. The general response is one of interest and pleasure, especially from the students who like the idea of pizza; there is some concern about time commitment, but eventually all ten faculty members agree to attend and a total of twenty four fellows and students are recruited. In this way, even with some no-shows, there should be a sufficient number of participants to ensure a productive discussion at each session.

With the date set and the participants contacted, the team members now turn their attention back to the questions. Using the project's goals as their base, they develop a list of specific questions, which they review for wording and clarity. They consider the order in which they want to ask the questions, knowing that it helps to start with a general one and then move into the more specific ones. They test the questions out on another librarian, only to find that in one or two cases they have not made the questions open enough for good discussion. They also decide on some prompts that will only be used if particular items are not brought up spontaneously by the participants, realizing that their not being mentioned might be significant. Their final list is as follows:

1. What uses do you currently make of the library's services and resources to further your research? PROMPTS: Having online literature searches provided by the library; using the library's book and journal collections; attending library classes in learning to search online databases and the Web; borrowing books and journals the library doesn't own; study space; access to Internet services; looking up information on the library's home pages; accessing online journals made available by the library.

2. How satisfied are you with the services/resources you use? [*Originally: Are you satisfied with the library's resources and services?*]

3. How could the library improve its current services/resources?

4. Given this special funding, which may not be repeated next year, what particular services/resources might the library add that will help your research?

5. How do you see your information needs and the ways you get that information changing in the future? [*Originally: Do you think the way you look for information is going to change much in the future?*]

6. When the library has something new you might want to know
about, how can we best reach you and others like you whose
names we may not know? PROMPTS: Individual e-mail messages;
e-mail discussion list; regular newsletters—print or electronic;
special mailings.

After discussing the questions with their library colleague and
revising them somewhat, as a final quality check, the team decides to
try out the questions on a postdoctoral fellow from another
department who is a frequent library user and well known by some
of the reference librarians.

In the meantime, the institute's conference room, adjacent to some
of the faculty offices is inspected and seems to be a suitable site for the
focus groups. Although the team would prefer a "neutral" location,
away from both the library and the institute, free rooms are difficult to
find at the university. Team members agree to compromise and opt for
a good, non-library location. The room houses a large table which can
seat up to sixteen people, with comfortable chairs. Although one wall
has several windows, the room is on the third floor, so is protected
from outside noise and distractions. The room is frequently used for
meetings and seminars, so can be closed off with a "meeting in
progress sign" to avoid interruptions. The library already owns a tape
recorder with a sensitive microphone, which when tested by the team,
is able to pick up voices from anywhere around the table.

Two days before the first discussion session participants are called
to remind them about the time and place. Eventually only eight of the
ten faculty attend, but the session turns out to be lively and
productive. On arrival, each member is greeted and given a name card
to fill-in and place in front of themselves on the table. This allows the
discussion leader and assistant to identify and refer to participants by
name, even though they are well known to each other. Before moving
into the first of the questions, the moderator thanks everyone for
coming and briefly explains the objectives and the fact that the session
is intended to generate ideas and information and is only one of three
which will be held. She states that while an important issue is how the
special funding might be used, the library is also eager to hear other
aspects of the faculty's information needs. She reminds participants of
the total amount of the money available and the fact that funding may
not be provided on an ongoing basis. Finally she stresses the importance of hearing their honest opinions and concerns; reminding them
that remarks will be taped to make sure that nothing is missed, but

that comments will not be attributed to any particular individual during the analysis and reporting of the project.

The discussion begins with a round of introductions that include a brief description of each person's research area. Again, the participants know one another, but this allows them to introduce themselves to the discussion leaders and helps to "breaks the ice." While the moderator goes through the questions and prompts for specific information at times, the other team member observes the group, making note of any overt behaviors which may have bearing on the discussion: strong feelings about a particular topic, in this case, a rather angry professor recalling long waits for ILL requests; interactions between two faculty members who seem to always disagree. Having name cards helps her to identify each person whom she observes, and her notes contain a brief mention of the topic that elicited the particular reaction or behavior noted. At the end of the session, which lasts just over one and a half hours, the moderator briefly sums up the main ideas that have emerged from the discussion. Most of the faculty express agreement, and one member adds a couple of thoughts. The moderator again thanks the faculty for attending and promises to share the outcome with them, including the specific decisions on how the special funding will be used. When the participants leave the team runs through the tapes to check for quality. They discuss their observations and make notes on their impressions and thoughts about the main ideas that emerged during the session. They agree that all the questions seem to have been understood, but note that the fifth question about future changes to information needs was not really needed since this information came out in the discussion from the previous two questions. They agree that this question might be safely discarded with the other groups depending on how the discussion progresses. Because the faculty have made several interesting suggestions on how money might be spent (*e.g.*, videotaping visiting seminar speakers for staff who are unable to attend the session, and making the tapes available on loan from the library), they decide to test these out on subsequent groups, after they have been given the opportunity of coming up with their own suggestions.

After the debriefing session, the tapes are then given to the administrative assistant to begin transcribing. Similar procedures are followed for the other two sessions. The second session attracts five students and only one postdoctoral fellow, and the library learns that a seminar organized by the biochemistry department, which they had not been aware of, had kept several people from attending. Because of this, when calls are made to the participants in the third group, the team members stress the importance of their attendance and double check that the time set is still a good one. The final discussion group is better attended, with eight students and four fellows, and turns out to be the most lively of the three. The suggestions made in earlier discussions are put forward to the second and third groups and prove to be a good stimulus for refinements and new ideas. The videotaping idea is universally applauded, but there is disagreement as to the importance of installing computers at the institute to provide easier access to library resources. While faculty were not very enthusiastic about this, the students and fellows think it is an excellent idea. Ideally, the students would like independent access to library facilities because they often work very late at night to get better access to equipment. Having computer access within the institute seems a good compromise suggestion. In spite of the librarian reminding everyone that the funding may only last one year, all three groups suggest the library use some of the funds to subscribe to new journals.

The team is now ready to begin the formal analysis of all the data. At the final debriefing, they review their comments from the previous sessions, which have been written up, and decide on the major themes that have emerged. They decide to both work through the transcript of the first session, independently, to identify and sort the data, and then compare their findings. They believe this will help provide a "reality check," allow for any necessary revisions to the categories and determination of any new themes that might emerge from a careful review of the data. Once this is completed, they will then each take one of the remaining sessions to analyze. The process of transcript and note reviewing, and listening to the tape of the first session proves to be a very challenging and time-consuming effort, but both agree that it helps them with the analysis of a second discussion. The final step includes a review of each major theme, in turn, looking at findings from each of the three groups, and drafting initial impressions and conclusions. Some major findings emerge, which are included in the report:

- Institute members seem very familiar with the major online databases and major resources in their field;
- Most participants are computer literate and don't hesitate to run their own searches but are sometimes frustrated with the results and could use some advice on good search strategy;
- Students and younger faculty are more comfortable with using computers and the Internet than some of the senior faculty;

- All express frustration with the time and effort needed in "weeding out" useless information from the Internet and would like help with this;

- Although many participants feel they need help with getting the best out of online resources, they are generally reluctant to take time to attend classes;

- Incoming graduate students, because they arrive with varying library knowledge and skills, need better orientation to the local library's resources and services, but this should be after the first couple of weeks of the quarter because of other needs;

- Many issues concerning library use are fairly mundane: concerns about finding the journal issue they want; frustration at the time needed to get an article from a journal the library does not own, but overall members express great appreciation for library resources and the help they get whenever they ask;

- Most members are unaware of the attempts the library has made to involve them in decision making about which journal subscriptions to cut and it appears that the library's methods of communicating with this group have not been adequate;

- Several specific ideas emerge about how the special funding should be used: taping seminar presentations so that those who cannot attend could view these at a later time; the need for more and better hardware to access eletronic resources, especially within the institute, which is located at a considerable distance from the library, so that members don't have to go to the library as much and compete with other users;

- Circulation of new journal issues from the library emerged as a hot topic because recent budget cuts within the institution forced the cancellation of some of their in-house subscriptions to a few heavily used journals.

The project team and library director review the final report and discuss the findings. They are generally pleased with the results, believe they have gained valuable insight into the group, and have some concrete ideas they can implement in terms of spending the special funds. They agree that the journal circulation issue is important and decide to look at this further, including other library users, perhaps with a survey. They decide to hold a small retreat with public service staff to discuss how best to provide assistance with search strategy and use of the Internet, since most focus group participants expressed reluctance to attend a class. The library director calls the head of the Timson Institute and briefly reviews the findings, while thanking her again for her cooperation. She says that a report will be sent to the head, as well as to those who attended the groups. The team members draft this report, which summarizes the major findings, briefly describes the areas for further investigation, and lists the decisions made on how the special funding will be used: purchasing two computers and printers, to be installed in one of the institute's rooms; beginning the seminar taping project; setting aside some funding for expedited ILL service and providing routine fax or electronic mail transmission of all articles to the institute; providing special classes, at the institute in Internet and online database search techniques; and identifying a specific individual as a liaison with institute members to help with search questions, hardware and software concerns, etc. The idea of providing independent access to graduate students after hours is rejected as incompatible with security concerns.

The Hospital Setting: St. George's is a relatively small hospital on the outskirts of a city that has a medical school. The hospital has recently embarked on three residency training programs: obstetrics/gynecology, emergency medicine, and orthopedics. Being situated as it is between the city and the rich farmlands that surround it, the hospital sees a good mix of cases, including a high number of agricultural accidents and births from within the farming community, many of which involve non-English-speaking migrant farmworkers' families. The library at the hospital is small (600 books and 70 journals, some of which are held in other departments) but has managed, in spite of recent cutbacks, to retain its full-time professional librarian. She is assisted by a part-time student, attending the local community college, and several volunteers, who work a varying number of hours. The hospital librarian is relatively new and is eager to learn more about the needs of her users. She is also aware that the new residency programs will place more demand on library resources. Among her various concerns, she is aware that although the library is open to everyone, nurses seem to make very little use of library services or resources. Coming from a previous position at an academic library, she has worked with nursing students and is knowledgeable about nursing resources. She feels certain that the hospital library can be more useful to the nursing staff here at St. George's, knows that at other institutions the nursing staff have been successfully encouraged to utilize library services more, and wants to be able to talk to the St. George staff about their information needs.

The librarian considers using a written survey, but decides she needs a more open means of learning about this group and its concerns. She decides that the focus group method may work better for her present needs. She has read one or two articles about the use of focus groups in libraries and is eager to see if the method will be useful in her setting. The student volunteer has taken a research methods class and has some familiarity with the focus group technique. In discussing the nurses' low use of the library, the two agree that this may be a useful approach; that they will develop some questions and lead some focus group discussions. If the sessions turn out to be a useful way to gather information, they will try the same approach with other hospital staff. The two of them will make up the "team" that will conduct the entire project. They decide that as a first step, the student will do some research on the focus group methodology when she is next on campus and bring in useful information for the librarian.

In doing her research, the student talks about the project with the faculty member from whom she has taken the research methods class. He is enthusiastic and offers advice as well as a promise to review the questions that are developed for the sessions. Armed with some articles and some useful tips from the professor, the student is eager to begin the project. She gives the articles to the librarian and they agree to meet the next week. At this meeting, the librarian states that she feels the focus group method will indeed be appropriate but is concerned that the project will involve a lot of time and effort and that she wants to feel more "comfortable" about using focus groups, before she commits herself. She informs the student that she will do some of her own research and they will meet again in a few days.

The librarian decides to call a colleague at the medical school library in town to discuss the proposed project and see if she can learn more practical details about using focus groups in the library setting. Her colleague is not familiar with the technique but puts her in touch with another librarian on staff who is. The hospital librarian contacts this person who, it turns out, has read about the methodology, has himself attended a focus group session, and knows of a hospital setting where focus groups have been used. He provides a name and telephone number and the librarian at St. George's is able to learn a great deal from this referral. In talking with the library manager who has experience with the technique, she also brings up her concerns about the nurses and asks about their library usage at this individual's institution. She learns that the focus group technique has been a very good way of hearing from the hospital staff, but that it was better when groups were not mixed, (*e.g.*, physicians made up a separate group from nurses, etc). She also hears similar concerns expressed about the under-utilization of the library by nurses and how the discussions in the groups illustrated a lot of misconceptions and lack of knowledge about services. The telephone discussion is very helpful; the librarian now feels more confident that the project is not only realistic, but necessary, and has a better idea of what is involved in terms of time and money. She also takes some time to review the nursing literature about information needs of nurses in the hospital setting, since this could help in developing the questions and in analyzing the results.

When the two team members meet at the end of the week, the student is excited to learn that the project will go forward. They review the librarian's original concerns about the nursing staff, look at some of the findings from the nursing literature, and develop some specific objectives for the project. These are:

- To better understand the information needs of working nurses;
- To learn more about the nurses' information seeking behavior;
- To identify barriers to the nurses' use of the library;
- To gather suggestions on how library services might be made more accessible to nurses.

They begin to develop these objectives into specific questions. At this meeting a list is made of all the tasks involved in the project, what expenses there might be, and whether or not they need anyone else to help them. They decide that in reality they cannot afford to spend very much money, and agree that a maximum of $50 should cover expenses for audiotapes and light refreshments. In terms of staffing, they decide they cannot involve the volunteers to any great extent. Because the discussions will almost certainly take place during working hours, someone will be needed to keep the library functioning during those times. Moreover, since the librarian feels that participants' responses should be kept confidential, she feels it best that the two of them be the only ones involved in the actual discussions. However, the librarian may be able to involve the volunteers in some aspects of the project and decide that whatever the volunteers' level of involvement, the librarian will inform them all of the impending project.

In dividing up duties, the two agree that the library manager will make the initial contact with the hospital's director of nursing to tell her about the project and that the library will be calling departmental nursing directors to ask for their assistance in selecting nurses. She will then contact the directors of the various hospital departments, including those in ambulatory care services, case management, operating rooms, wards, intensive care, and education services for help in identifying staff. Once this is completed, the student will contact individual nurses for screening and recruiting. They decide to share the duties of moderating because both wish to gain experience with the technique. A total of four discussion groups is planned. Analysis of individual discussions will also be shared and the student will put together overall conclusions from the different groups.

The initial meeting with the nursing director goes well. She is enthusiastic about the project but cautions the librarian that it may be difficult to recruit nurses because of their busy schedules. When the departmental directors are contacted, most of them also express enthusiasm and while one director provides some specific names of possible participants, most refer the librarian to the nursing secretary for a list of staff. The secretary, who has been at the hospital many years, proves to be very helpful and provides other useful information about nursing work schedules, meetings, and other obligations that might impact the dates and times of sessions.

Before her next meeting with the student, the librarian begins to think about a suitable site and decides that the hospital administration's conference room would be ideal if they can use it. She calls the administrative office, explains her need, and gets approval. She writes down the room schedule for the next month and agrees to call back the next day with six dates, which will be blocked out for library use. She is relieved that the room is often available in the early evening because this may be a better time for some nurses to attend a discussion, when their shifts are over. When the team members meet they check their calendars and the limitations on availability of the nurses, and select six tentative dates for potential discussion sessions. They review the questions they have drafted and discuss possible improvements. The student decides to take a copy of them to share with her professor.

Meanwhile, in discussing who to recruit and how groups might be structured, the team members wonder if it might be effective to divide the groups by duty since this may effect their information needs. For example, all nurses in ambulatory care would form one group, while nurses from the wards and intensive care units would be in another. On the other hand, they both think that it would be important not to mix users with non-users. They realize it may be difficult to arrange groups given these parameters, and decide to begin making calls and see what sort of response they get from the different departments, and what percentage of those contacted are non-users. They also agree that all participants should have worked at the hospital for at least six months, so that they are familiar with their work routine and with the layout of the hospital. The two decide on some simple screening questions to discover how much the nurses have used the library and how long they have been at the hospital. During the screening, the intent is also to encourage the nurses to talk about themselves so that the student can form some opinion of their ability to participate in active discussion. Other than this, they feel that no other criteria are needed to select participants.

The student finds that although almost all the nurses contacted are intrigued by the project and want to participate, many of them cannot come to a discussion at any of the available times because of their work schedule and family responsibilities; others have very limited times when they could attend. After several calls, the student meets with the librarian to review the situation. They agree that grouping nurses by duty is not as important as getting a sufficient number together at the same time for a discussion! The student then proceeds through the list, annotating names with comments about their library use, interest level, and availability, as well as their ability to be forthcoming and articulate during the conversation. Of those who are able to attend, the majority have used the library at least once and represent most of the hospital departments. After contacting almost everyone included, she arrives at four good dates and a list of some thirty individuals who are able to attend at least one of these, including eight non-users. Most of the nurses who are interested in the project are quite happy and willing to talk to the student, so she feels that the discussions will be productive. However, the whole experience is a long and frustrating one and at the conclusion, the student realizes that there are no representatives from two of the hospital departments. Given the difficulties in getting any commitments, the librarian decides to proceed with the groups as constituted. In looking over the student's notes, it seems that there are nurses in each of these two departments who would be willing to participate but cannot make any of the dates. The team decides to use a modified strategy and conduct individual interviews with a representative from each of the departments, so that all areas of the hospital are covered.

In returning to the questions, the team review the comments made by the college professor. He has made some suggestions for wording changes so that questions don't encourage just a "yes" or "no" answer. He also feels that they may have too many questions and has illustrated how several of their shorter questions can be drawn into larger, more general ones. For example, their questions about specific problems with using the library are developed into a single one that allows the nurses to describe their own problems, rather than reacting to things the library staff perceive as being problems. Based on the results of their recruitment efforts, the team decides to hold three user groups and one non-user group. Following are the final questions for the two groups, along with some possible prompts to bring out specific items, and the original wording:

- When you have an information question on the job, where do you go for an answer and why? (both)

- When would you consider going to the hospital's library for information? (both) How often does this happen? (users); how often might this happen? (non-users) [*Originally: How often do you use the library?*]

- When you do go to the library, what resources have you found there which can help answer your questions? (users)

- Given the questions which come up on the job, how do you think the library might help you answer them? (non-users)

- Which of these have you found the most/least useful in answering your questions, and why? (users)

- What other resources would you like to see the library provide? (users) [*Originally: Do you need anything else to answer your questions?*]

- What do you see as the biggest barriers which prevent you from using the library when you need information? (both) [*Originally: Are library hours sufficient for your needs? What sort of assistance do you need when you come to the library? What training do you need to make it easier to use library resources on your own? How big a factor is cost when you need information?*]

  PROMPTS: Time, cost of service, hours library is open, distance from worksite, difficulties in using library resources, lack of trained staff to help you in the library.

- Can you describe the perfect library for your nursing needs? (both)

A tape recorder is acquired from the medical records department and arrangements are made with the cafeteria to provide coffee, tea, and cookies at the discussions. The librarian agrees to lead the first two groups, with the student observing and acting as a back-up moderator; for the next two groups they will switch roles. Library volunteers are recruited to call each individual the day before the discussion at which they are scheduled to attend. During these calls, directions are given to the conference room. Each potential attendee is strongly encouraged to attend and the importance of their participation is emphasized. Volunteers learn that two of the potential attendees have had a change in schedule and will not be able to attend.

Eventually, six people attend the first session, ten show up for the second, and another nine come to the third. Seven of the eight non-users show up for their session. The first one gets off to a slow start but the nurses and the moderator eventually warm up and a good discussion ensues. The participants seem very enthusiastic and when all the questions have been answered several express their pleasure that the library staff have shown this much interest in their needs. Some word must have been spread to other nurses because ten people come to the second group and the discussion is animated. After each session, the team members check that the recorder picked up all the conversation, review the discussion, and record their impressions of any important non-verbal behaviors, as well as the major outcomes from the group. Three issues stand out in all four groups: surprise that the library is in fact open to nurses because this had not been the case at other institutions in which they had worked; lack of awareness of even the basic services provided by the library; and concern that regardless of the services offered, nurses have little opportunity to use the library except "on their own time."

Both the librarian and student feel that the discussions have been worthwhile and that valuable information has been learned. The student volunteers to transcribe the first tape and both team members then review the transcript and listen to the tape. The student offers to go through the transcript and organize the data. This proves to be very time consuming but is useful in identifying the major discussion categories and grouping comments under each. Most of the categories correspond to the questions asked, however, some new ideas emerge and become additional categories, (*e.g.*, the nurses' concerns about the information needs of their patients; their bad experiences with some library volunteers). They agree to handle the second tape differently. They copy each category identified from the first group onto large sheets of butcher paper. Then together they listen to the tape, stopping after each speaker to write up the ideas on the appropriate sheet. Any new ideas or opinions that don't fit into the existing categories are written onto separate sheets. This turns out to be a successful method and they proceed with the third and fourth tapes. When all the tapes have been reviewed and the information grouped, the student synthesizes all the comments about each category. Both team members review this write up and discuss what they have learned, as well as the implications. They realize that while there are some differences in information needs and practices among nurses from different departments, many of the concerns are the same. The following major ideas emerge:

- Many patients speak Spanish and nurses need more resources for themselves to communicate with their patients;

- Patients need more information about their own health problems and taking care of themselves and their children and nurses would like to see these available in the hospital library;

- Nurses don't all know that the library is available to them;

- There is a real need for the library to be open longer in the evening because of nurses' working hours;

- Given limited opportunities/time to use the library, more efficient means to use it would be most valuable;

- More resources are needed at nursing stations;

- Most nurses need help searching and looking things up;

- Many nurses are not happy with some of the volunteers who work in the library because they cannot provide the level of assistance they need;

- An orientation and welcome to the library would be very helpful for new nurses even if this is just a brief tour and reassurance that they are welcome;

- Nurses rely heavily on their colleagues in Education Services for information needs, since they are more accessible than the library;

- Library staff should work closely with nurse educators, providing these individuals with in-depth training because they then go on to train the nurses.

Given the results of the focus group discussions the librarian makes some decisions. Several changes can be made quickly, others need more long-range planning. In the short term, she decides to investigate resources for nurses in Spanish and include funding for these materials in her next budget. She develops a brief orientation and welcome packet for new nursing staff. She also develops a new orientation and training plan for library volunteers, which emphasizes the importance of referring more difficult questions to her. A meeting is scheduled with the chief nursing administrator to discuss some of the results and their implications. These include: how to incorporate a library orientation into the hospital's own orientation for new hires; whether the hospital might want to investigate ways to make information available at nursing stations; and what plans the hospital might have to provide patient education materials. Another meeting is scheduled with the staff development personnel to discuss some possible training classes for them in information access.

Meanwhile, the librarian and student write letters to each of the nurses who attended the discussions to thank them for their participation and send them a brief report of the major findings. The letter indicates the decisions made by the librarian and the actions taken or planned as a result of the discussions. Overall the focus group project has been rewarding, though both team members agree that it was more difficult than they imagined. They also agree, however, that hearing directly from their users is extremely useful and the librarian believes that the methodology can be useful with other groups. The student feels she gained good experience in moderating the sessions and in analyzing the data.

Lessons Learned: These two case studies, one in a hospital, the other in an academic health center, have been used to illustrate both the steps taken and the issues involved in running a focus group project in a busy, functioning library. The two case studies provide practical insight into the value and use of the technique. In spite of the differences in their setting and objectives, and in the participants involved, they share some common lessons that can serve librarians in all types of libraries who wish to plan and conduct projects using the focus group methodology.

- The focus group methodology was correctly selected as the most appropriate of several methods of data gathering to answer the information need in a particular case.

- In-house staff successfully ran the project because individuals were selected who had enthusiasm for the topic and/or the methodology and who had the right potential for moderating and for carefully analyzing the results.

- Out-of-pocket expenses were relatively low, but staff time was considerable and should be considered a hidden cost.

- The library director had to "buy in" to the project to ensure the necessary commitment of money and time, and to guarantee the ultimate use of the project's findings.

- Partnering with others, either outside or within the institution, helped in many important functions: selection of good participants, promotion of the project, testing potential questions, access to a "neutral" site.

- Pre-planning was extensive but paid off with good results.

- Questions were improved by "field-testing."

- Participant selection was important; while some common characteristics are essential for a good discussion, flexibility about others may be necessary.

- Although a truly neutral location was not available, using a room outside the library and out of the participants' daily work environment helped focus attention on the discussion.

- Timing of the discussion to fit with the participants' schedules and routines helped ensure that people showed up.

- When key individuals could not attend a session, and their voices needed to be heard, individual interviews were used as an alternative method. The focus group does not have to be an exclusive approach.

- Planning needed to be flexible enough to accommodate the realities of the participants' job responsibilities and schedules.

- People did not all show up even though they said they would. Other factors may turn out to be more important to them.

- An observer offered important additional information to enrich the analysis. Running a focus group is itself a group activity.

- Questions often need to be modified during the project if they turn out to be ambiguous or repetitive.

- Important new ideas may emerge from the first discussion and then can be tested out on later groups. The focus group project is dynamic.

- Analysis was time-consuming but became easier with succeeding sessions.

- Follow-up was important so that participants were assured that their contributions had been heard and that the project accomplished its objectives.

Resources

꧁꧂

General Texts and Articles:

Advertising Research Foundation. Focus groups: issues and approaches. New York: The Foundation, 1985.

Aubel J. Guidelines for studies using the group interview technique. Geneva: United Nations, International Labour Office, 1994.

Calder BJ. Focus groups and the nature of qualitative marketing research. J Market Res 1977;14:353–64.

Gordon W, Langmaid R. Qualitative market research: a practitioner's and buyer's guide. Aldershot, England: Gower, c1988.

Focus Group Kit. Thousand Oaks, CA: Sage Publications, 1998. 6 vols.

Greenbaum TL. The handbook for focus group research. New York: Lexington Books, 1993.

Holloway I, Wheeler, S. Qualitative research for nurses. Oxford: Blackwell Scientific, 1996.

Krueger RA. Focus groups: a practical guide for applied research. 2nd ed. Thousand Oaks, CA: Sage Publications, 1994.

Merton RK, Fiske M, Kendall PL. The focused interview: a manual of problems and procedures. 2nd ed. New York: Macmillan, 1990.

Morgan DL. Focus groups as qualitative research. 2nd ed. Thousand Oaks, CA: Sage Publications, 1997.

Morgan DL, ed. Successful focus groups: advancing the state of the art. Newbury Park, CA: Sage Publications, 1993.

Vaughn S, Schumm JS, Sinagub J. Focus group interviews in education and psychology. Thousand Oaks, CA: Sage Publications, 1996.

Wells WD. Group interviewing. In: Ferber R., ed. Handbook of marketing research. New York: McGraw Hill, 1974:2–142.

Understanding qualitative research. New York: Advertising Research Foundation, 1992.

Library Applications:

Connaway LS. Focus group interviews: a data collection methodology for decision making. Libr Admin & Man 1996 Fall;10(4):231–9.

Glitz B. The focus group technique in library research: an introduction. Bull Med Libr Assoc 1997 Oct;85(4):385–90.

Mullaly-Quijas P, Ward DH, Woelfl N. Using focus groups to discover health professionals' information needs: a regional marketing study. Bull Med Libr Assoc 1994 July;82(3):305–11.

Robbins K, Holst R. Hospital library evaluation using focus group interviews. Bull Med Libr Assoc 1990 July; 78(3):311–3.

Wagner MM, Mahmoodi SH. A focus group interview manual. New York: American Library Association, Continuing Library Education Network and Exchange Round Table, 1994.

ANALYSIS:

Miles MB, Huberman AM. Qualitative data analysis: an expanded sourcebook. 2nd ed. Thousand Oaks, CA: Sage Publications, c1994.

Tesch R. Qualitative research: analysis types and software tools. New York: Falmer Press, 1990.

INDEX